In loving memory of

William Richard Maxwell

1953 to 1989

Suicide

Living With the Question

Ruth H. Maxwell

authorHOUSE®

AuthorHouse™
1663 Liberty Drive
Bloomington, IN 47403
www.authorhouse.com
Phone: 1-800-839-8640

Published by AuthorHouse   06/01/2012

ISBN: 978-1-4685-5592-9 (sc)
ISBN: 978-1-4685-5591-2 (e)

Library of Congress Control Number: 2012903147

Acknowledgments

I could not have completed this project without the help and support of many. Their gentle feedback, loving encouragement, and steadfast loyalty has enriched my life. Heartfelt gratitude to Allison Beezer, Elsa Bowman, Paul Carlo, Nancy Cochran, Dennis and Cheryl DuRoff, Judi and Len Hanson, Dan Haygeman, Jake Hufft, Sat Kahr Khalsa, Phoebe Kitanidis, Judy MacCready, Jennifer and Carter Mackley, Patricia Mauser McCord, R. Patrick Neary, Albert Ogle, Michael Reandeau, Merle Richlen, Mark Shimada, Abigail Spellman, Cynthia Whitcomb, and Laura Whitcomb. A special thank you to Jeanne Gransee Barker for ideas for the cover, and to Werner Erhard for the *est* training.

I am especially grateful for my family—children, grandchildren, great grandchildren, and my extended family. They are a blessing and the joy of my life.

Prologue

We live in a culture that worships youth, a land of opportunity where everything is possible. Death is treated as an aberration and we find it easier to mask it and deny the inevitability of it.

When an older person dies, we grieve, but knowing it was time for them to go comforts our sorrow. When a younger person dies, the universe loses all credibility, and the old orders seem to crumble. To have that person die by his or her own hand is bizarre, beyond our understanding. There is no format for dealing with such an issue, and the mourners left behind feel not only their grief, but also guilt and abandonment. The rules have been broken. The word is whispered, "suicide." Euphemisms are used, "took his own life," "ended it all." Questions are in everyone's eyes. Denial and secrecy become the new mode, acid added to the open wound of grief, and a code of silence is begun.

Ten days before his 36th birthday, my son Bill committed suicide. There were no obvious reasons. This was not a boy with a drug problem or a young man with a broken heart, not someone defeated by life. This was a man, handsome and smart, married to a beautiful loving woman, father to two adorable boys, beginning what was expected to be a profitable career in his dream job with the company he had chosen. He was successful, loved, had found his place in life.

My grief was brutal, rock-hard, stripped of all but the raw reality of death. I felt my heart had been torn from my body. I wanted to drop out of living, to never have to exert myself in any way ever again. My heart could not stop wondering why. I desperately needed to find the answer. My life, my sanity hung in the balance.

Several weeks after his death, I made an appointment with a psychiatrist. She listened patiently, asked a few questions, and at the end of our session asked if she could take a little more of my time. I was puzzled, but agreed. "What have you done to stay so sane?" she asked.

I was surprised. I hadn't felt particularly sane, more like a zombie, just managing to put one foot in front of the other. But she had noticed something, so I looked to see how I had been functioning. What had I done? She waited patiently while I thought. Gradually, I realized I had done two things. One, in Werner Erhard's seminars (est), I had learned the difference between the words "and" and "but." That word "but" negates the statement. "He was a wonderful man, <u>but</u> he committed suicide." The "but" negates all the wonderfulness of the man. I no longer thought like that. I no longer demanded that life be black or white. I had learned to live with two diametrically opposed thoughts at the same time. I knew my son was one of the most responsible people I had ever known <u>and</u> he had committed one of the most irresponsible acts. I did not have to deny my son to admit the truth of his suicide. At the same time, I did not have to deny the suicide to have my wonderful son. Both of those statements were true and I live with both equally.

The second thing was also something I had learned in my est Training. I physically allowed myself to experience my feelings, noting where in my body they were occurring, allowing them to be until they dissipated. Feelings are like lightning. They'll go through anything, even you, to get grounded. And until they are grounded, they live in your body causing all manner of mischief. I was terrified at first to allow the feelings to have sway over me for I feared they would kill me. I often waited until I was alone to experience them, for sometimes the intensity of my grief astounded me. Screaming and acting out do *not* let you experience the feelings on a physical level. The feelings are internal, in your physical body. It's a matter of being conscious—aware—of your body and consciously watching and allowing what happens. And sometimes you scream.

I am a product of our Western culture, one that believes strongly in cause and effect. There are reasons for everything, and if we don't know them, we will search diligently until we find them. Something, someone *has* to be to blame. I knew there had to be some answers and so I began to research. I read everything I could get my hands on. There was no Internet then and so I combed the library. As of today, I've read over fifty books plus numerous articles and still I search. I've talked with a number of experts. And I now have some opinions on the subject.

Suicide is still taboo. We aren't that removed from the old notions about suicide—that it's a crime. There was a time when people who tried but failed to kill themselves were arrested and thrown into jail. As if they hadn't suffered enough. Historically, people who committed suicide were not allowed burial in sacred ground. Their bodies were buried beneath the intersection of a crossroad so their souls could never find their way to heaven, doomed to roam for eternity.

We, my family and I, were fortunate. My son left a poem for us with his suicide letter, and we used it to create the context within which to hold his death. Rainer Maria Rilke, a German poet who suffered from clinical depression, wrote the poem.

> *Be patient toward all that is unsolved in your heart*
> *And try to love the questions themselves.*
> *Do not now seek the answers that cannot be given you*
> *because you would not be able to live them.*
> *And the point is to live everything.*
> *Live the questions now.*
> *Perhaps you will gradually,*
> *without noticing it,*
> *live along some distant day*
> *into the answer.*

My purpose in writing this book was twofold. One, I found it therapeutic to be able to record our experiences. Two, it is my opinion that our Western society needs to begin the conversation about suicide as a subject all by itself. Now it's usually tacked onto the talk about depression. However, not all depressed individuals consider suicide and many who do take their own lives are not depressed. With the return of so many from the current battlefields, the rates of suicide are growing in an alarming fashion. We need to do all we can for those suffering from post-traumatic stress disorder and from the horrors of war.

Suicide is usually found in the broad field of "mental illness." "He wasn't himself," they say. My question then is: Who was he?

Just as alcoholism has been lifted into the light out of the morass of moral weakness, we must find ways to shine the light of openness on the subject of suicide to bring understanding and compassion to all. Let's live with and talk about the questions so that we may someday be able to grow into answers.

I've never been able to resolve Bill's suicide, close the door on it, wipe my hands and say, "That's that." It's what we think we should do—complete it so we can move on. Put it all behind us. I have no wish to do that, and I have learned to live in peace and with an active, alive sense of Bill's presence. For me it is the only way. I must live fully in the present and part of that presence is the death of a son. We have all recovered as well as anyone can from the death of a loved one, and life is going on strongly in us all. This book is about our quest to continue to live the questions. It has taken years for me to write, for the wound of his death is tender still. But there has been healing for me in the writing. My hope is there will be comfort and healing for those who read.

Seattle, Washington
March 2012

Chapter One

On March 2nd, 1989, my son Bill rose at 5 am. His wife Laura didn't notice, for in the night their two-year-old son had tiptoed in, and asked her to sleep with him in his new big bed. This was only the second time in their marriage that Bill and Laura hadn't awakened together. The first time was when their elder son needed comforting in his "grown-up" bed a few years earlier. Bill had dressed quietly, and left his house in Santa Monica.

The raucous cries of parrots woke me at 5:00 that morning in Pasadena. The flock of Patagonian condors liked the tall pecan trees that bordered my yard. They often woke me, those noisy wild birds. I usually enjoyed them, but not this morning. My head throbbed with the worst headache I had ever had.

There was no going back to sleep, so I rose, showered and dressed. I puttered about in my office, getting notes together for a consulting job later that morning, but I had trouble concentrating. I was out of sorts, discombobulated, as my father would say.

My phone rang at 9:00. It was Laura. She sounded concerned. "Ruth, has Bill called you?"

"No."

"He's not at work," she said. In their eight years together that had never happened, not even with his serious bout with bronchitis, from which he was still not recovered. He was always at work—the first to arrive, the last to leave.

"Anything wrong?" I asked.

"I'm not sure. If he calls, talk to him, then ask him to call me."

"Okay, Laura. I will."

I was puzzled, but not concerned. I know Los Angeles traffic. Anything's liable to happen. I also knew Bill. He was the most responsible person I knew.

1

Something had come up, I was sure. He'd call her soon. I said goodbye, hung up, and went to take another aspirin.

As I drove to my consulting job, I smiled as I thought of this son. He had helped me plan the training I was doing for this staff of people who worked with seriously abused children. I had promised to report on how it went. Where had the time gone, I wondered? It seemed like only yesterday I was a mother with four little kids. Now they were all grown and gone. Bill, child number three, had a birthday coming up in ten days. He'd be thirty-six. I wondered what kind of celebration we'd have.

His birthday was always special for me, as I was not supposed to have him. The doctors had warned me not to have another pregnancy. Something to do with my RH factor. I had another son (John) and a daughter (Mary). As far as my mother and mother-in-law were concerned, I should have been content. But I wanted another baby.

The pregnancy with Bill was unusual. I gained five pounds the first month, something I had never done before. And then gained again the second month. "Well," my obstetrician said, "if this continues, we'll take pictures. Any twins in your family?" But in my third month we moved away. I did a lot of bleeding, but that had happened during my pregnancy with Mary. At that time the doctor had said to "just take it easy." I did and Mary was a healthy baby. So I found a new doctor in our new town. He was a bit intimidating, a Dr-God-kind of person, so I didn't even bother to tell him about the bleeding and cramps. All seemed well. I was busy fixing up a new home and trying to be a loving wife and caring mother.

This move was to a suburb of Minneapolis. We bought a house out in the boonies, the first in a new development. There were no roads to speak of, just dirt tracks. No phone lines. The sound of hammers and saws everywhere as new houses went up around us. One afternoon, as I trudged out to pick up the mail, a carpenter approached.

"Hi, Missus," he said.

He took off his cap, and in his Norwegian accent said, "You are not to worry. We draw straws every morning to see who will take you to the hospital when your time comes."

I was touched by his sincere concern and knew they all dreaded pulling the short straw.

The circumstances around Bill's birth were almost like in the "olden days." The phone lines had not as yet come into this new development and we had only one car, which my husband Dick took to work every day. I wondered about those pioneer women. They'd done this. I could too. So I made arrangements with my friend Taffy to take John (5) and Mary (3) when the time came. I had a basket for each child with a change of clothes and favorite toys. I put them by the front door. We rehearsed what to do so we'd be ready. The night finally came and I got my little ones out of bed. They put on their snowsuits and mittens, for it was March, and stood sleepily by the door. Dick drove us to Taffy's house. I used her telephone to call my doctor, and left a message with his answering service. John and Mary stretched out on Taffy's sofa and were soon sound asleep. I kissed them, and Dick and I drove to the hospital.

Maternity wards in those days accommodated nurses and doctors. Expectant mothers were herded into "lying-in" rooms to wait alone until they were ready for delivery. Husbands were consigned to a waiting room and expected to pace and smoke cigars while they waited in suspense. Dick hated this business of my going off alone to deliver babies. It was my fourth trip. The third baby had died in utero. We did not want to go through that again. The nurses held off for as long as they could, waiting for my doctor to come from his party. Finally they could wait no longer and I was wheeled into the delivery room. A young physician entered the room. He'd been serving a mission in Africa and had returned to the states for further training. As I was being strapped down (they did that in those days) I extended my hand. "Excuse me," I said. I was not about to let a stranger deliver this baby. "I don't believe we've met."

He turned to the nurse. "Has she had a lot of anesthetic?"

The nurse shook her head. "None. Her doctor doesn't believe in any kind of pain medication."

He grinned, took my hand, and told me his name. "Now, let's deliver this baby."

We chatted during the breaks in labor. I remember telling this young doctor that God was kind to give us little breathers between contractions. I could bear the pain knowing there was an end to it.

And there was. "It's a boy," the doctor cried.

"What big feet!" said a nurse, and we all laughed. He was big, over eight pounds, with golden curls all over his head. *He looks like an angel*, I thought. We named him William for Dick's childless uncle and Richard for all the male Maxwells that had preceded him.

The only problem Bill had, a severe jaundice, soon disappeared, and he flourished. He did all his life. He was always beautiful, strong, and healthy.

And stubborn. This child had a will the likes of which I had never seen. He walked before he was ten months old, and would not hold your hand. He could get into anything, on top of everything, and had a mind of his own. I thought we would never get through the "two's"—those years of the "no." But I hung in there for I knew some day he'd be bigger than me and I wanted our relationship to be very clear. I was the mother and he the child.

The stubbornness finally grew into a quiet kind of strength.

I parked my car in the client's parking lot and shut off the engine. I was early and could take a little power nap so leaned back against the seat and closed my eyes. But sleep would not come. My mind was full of thoughts of Bill, of memories happy and sad. I thought about my marriage. I had loved my husband, and knew he loved me, but after twenty-five years of marriage, I could no longer stay. I knew the children were old enough to accept the changes. They not only approved, but had encouraged me to leave. John and Mary were well established on their own. Bill at nineteen was in college, Doug at eighteen fresh out of high school. So I left Dick and moved into a tiny apartment in Pasadena. Somehow we'd all survived.

For years, Bill and I had supported each other with weekly business meetings on the phone. We reported on how our work was going, goals accomplished or abandoned, along with new goals. It was really nice to have my children now be peers. I was still the "mom," but we had all become friends and the support was a blessing. It was also an eye-opener. Once, after a three-month trial of an organizational system Bill had given me, he asked how it was going. "The system doesn't work," I told him. He laughed. "That system works, Mom. You don't." I laughed with him, for he was right! I was the bottleneck in that program. It was easy to take correction from Bill, as his manner was direct but always gentle.

Bill was the one I began complaining to about being over-worked. I'd gone back to school to get graduate degrees, had a full-time job managing the twelve educators who worked at my tutorial business, and was spending about twenty hours a week doing volunteer work. That work was deeply satisfying as I saw individuals transform their lives, but with four hours of sleep a night, my health was beginning to suffer, and a whine I didn't like had shown up in my voice.

Bill asked how it was going and I told him I'd been asked to volunteer and lead another seminar.

There was a long pause, and then Bill spoke. "Mom, you can't be trusted around transformation. You need to learn how to say no. My advice, don't say 'yes' until you *tell* me first. I didn't say 'ask,' I said 'tell.'"

I agreed and it made a huge difference. In many ways, Bill seemed mature beyond his years. He was a good worker. All of my children were. And he had succeeded at everything he tried. Now he had his dream job and was greatly appreciated by his boss Terry.

I thought about Bill's work history. Although interested in art, his jobs had been based on his ability to do logistics and produce big events. One of his early jobs was with The Hunger Project under Albie Rosenhaus. When Albie went to MGM as vice president, he took Bill with him as his assistant. From there Bill went to New York where he produced large events for Werner Erhard, the founder of est, and worked for the author Tom Jackson, running his workshops. Bill thought nothing of managing events in Madison Square Garden. On his return to Los Angeles, he had several jobs, always with the dream of working for a major movie studio—one that matched his high standards. Now he had that job at Imagine Films.

My thoughts turned to Laura. I loved her like a daughter and was thrilled to have her in our lives. She and Bill had lived together in West Hollywood early on in their relationship, then decided to separate. Laura moved to New York. Bill stayed in Los Angeles. Several years passed, and then Bill decided to try his luck in the Big Apple, but we all suspected he wanted to be near Laura again. Before long he was calling to report how much he enjoyed being with Laura.

The day soon came when Bill's happy voice on my message tape said, "Call me, Mom. I've got some news."

I called. "What's up?" I asked.

"I'm engaged!"

I cheered.

They chose to be married in California where their families lived. The night before the wedding, we held a family dinner party at my small home. When it was time for all to leave, Laura's father brought Bill's suitcase in. Laura smiled. "We thought he should spend the night in your home." I was moved to tears by the thoughtful gesture. The next morning, Bill's brothers and sister helped him get ready and as a family we drove to the church.

Two years later, Laura was pregnant and they moved back to California to be close to their families. But now, this son who had grown into this confident, thoughtful man had not shown up at work. What on earth was

Bill doing this morning, I wondered? Was something wrong with his current project? Was he still as devoted to taking care of his spiritual life as he was to caring for his family and work? Perhaps he had gone somewhere to meditate. Or maybe there had been an accident. I was sure something had happened to delay him. I spent the day taking aspirin for the headache and meeting with clients.

When I returned home at 3:00 there were messages. I listened to the first and no others. The voice was Laura's piercing cry, "Ruth, call me!"

Chapter Two

To this day I hear the echo of that call in my mind—Laura's keening cry. That sound women have made down through the centuries. I was puzzled, for Laura, always so calm and centered, sounded frantic. I picked up the phone and called.

Laura's mother, Eugenia, answered. Her voice sounded flat, artificial. In a measured tone she said Laura had gotten a letter from Bill. Doug (my youngest son) and Bill's boss Terry had taken Laura to the police department to file a missing person complaint.

I listened to all of this academically. A letter? What kind of letter? And why a missing person complaint? I was so dumbfounded I couldn't even ask any questions.

"Wait at home, Ruth. They'll call you."

I hung up in a daze. Who were "they?" Why a phone call? What was going on? I had to do something while I waited for the call, but what? I couldn't seem to get my mind in gear. A package had come from my daughter. I set it aside. *Later*, I thought. I tried opening a file on my computer, but was too agitated to concentrate. I picked up the plastic letter opener Bill had made for me and bit my lip as I tried to remember: was he in the seventh or eighth grade? It seemed important that I remember. I felt a sudden desperate urge to hold tight to every memory of him.

The letter opener is half blue, half clear plastic and smooth to the touch. Bill had made it in junior high school. During that time, one afternoon Doug came home right after school, an unusual occurrence. "Bill said I shouldn't tell you, but I think you need to know," he said.

"What?" I asked.

"The coach calls him 'Fatso' and makes him run extra laps. Then Bill's late to his English class."

When I confronted Bill about it, he said to leave it alone, not do anything. "It's cool," he said. "I'll handle it."

But I knew he wouldn't. I told his father and we had a conference with the dean of the school. The hazing stopped.

I had accepted a job that year, teaching second grade in a pilot program in a new school just several blocks from our home. I loved it. My husband was nervous about my working outside of the home, but the kids thought it a great experiment. They helped me grade homework papers and gave me ideas for lesson plans. The school secretary had to remind me to pick up my check. *I get paid to do this?* I thought. Cool!

One afternoon, while teaching a lesson, I mentioned to my class that I had two sons in junior high school. "Oh," Danny spoke out. "We know your boys."

"You do?"

"Yeah. They came by one afternoon and said that if we ever gave you any trouble they would clean our clocks."

I was horrified and went to my principal. "Shirley," I said, "a horrible thing has happened." I told her what my sons had done. She laughed. "I think it's great," she said. "The kids do too, I'm sure. Shows your sons really love you."

Tears came to my eyes as I remembered the incident. My sons, so compassionate and thoughtful. But that same month I came home one afternoon earlier than usual. "I'm home," I called out. Something we all did as we entered the house. I stood at the bottom of the stairs and wrinkled my nose at a strong unfamiliar smell.

Mary, then sixteen, rushed up to me. "Mom, you've got to do something about Bill. He's going to kill himself."

"What's wrong?" I asked.

Then she told me.

I raced up the stairs and opened Bill's bedroom door. He was in his closet, his head in a plastic bag, the smell of airplane glue overwhelming. *Oh my God*, I thought, *he'll kill himself*. I grabbed him and hugged him as if to protect him from some evil beyond my understanding. "What are you doing?" I asked, over and over.

He gave no answer.

When his father came home, he yelled and spanked. "How could you do this?" he said over and over. "You'll kill yourself." But Bill had nothing to say in his defense.

"It's like he wants to get caught," I said.

"He does," my eldest son, John, said quietly.

Another day, a cold winter afternoon, I had been home only a few minutes when the phone rang.

"Mrs. Maxwell?" a male voice asked.

"Yes."

"Sergeant Schneider of the police force here."

My heart jolted.

"Do you have a son Bill?"

I mumbled I did.

"We've got him down here at the station."

I was numb with shock. I could not believe what I was hearing. "Is he all right?"

"Look," the sergeant said. "I'm going to be straight with you. We picked him up for shoplifting, but it was obvious he wanted to get caught. Is there some kind of trouble at home?"

"I . . . I . . . I don't think so."

"Well, I'm sending him home with a warning. We see this sort of thing all the time. Kids crying out for help. He seems to be a nice kid. Doesn't talk much. I think you should get some kind of counseling."

"For him?"

There was a pause. "No. I think family counseling."

His words struck a deep chord in me.

"I'll drive him home. I want to talk to him."

Bill was pale when he walked into the house. I did the parent thing—trying to get him to explain. He was sorry he had scared us. Beyond that he had little to say.

Those years were hard for both Doug and Bill. At thirteen and fourteen they were beginning to try to push the limits. Dick was crazy about their behavior, helpless in the face of it. One evening he and I went to a Downeast crab cookout at a neighbor's. Dick had been taking diet pills and after a few martinis began acting in a wild manner. He said he was going home and was I coming with him? I said no, and I stayed. When I got home a couple of hours later, the house felt too quiet. I started to go upstairs and saw a smashed TV set at the bottom of the stairs. What on earth could have happened, I wondered and raced up the stairs. I opened the door to Doug's room. The look on his face was one of terror.

"What happened?" I asked.

9

"Dad's crazy, berserk. He threw the TV down the stairs." Then he told me that Dick had gone into Bill's room, hit Bill and backed him into the corner. "You're king of the creeps," he said. "You'll never amount to anything." He hit him again and walked away.

Doug pointed to his wall. There was the print of a shoe.

I felt sick, nauseated. I hugged Doug and told him I'd take care of it. Then I went to Bill. He was in bed. I went to hug him. "Are you all right?" I asked.

He nodded. "I'm okay."

"Want to talk about it."

He shook his head. He never mentioned that incident and I wondered if there were others I knew nothing about.

I went downstairs. Dick had passed out in his red leather chair. I remember crying. This handsome successful man was destroying his children. I had to do something.

The next morning Dick was up and out of the house earlier than usual. I was sure he had no memory of what had happened. After dinner I asked him to go to our bedroom so we could talk. "We need to find a therapist," I said.

Dick looked surprised. "What for?"

"For us, you and me."

"Why?"

"Because of what happened last night," I said.

He was puzzled. "Last night?"

"Yes, and Bill's shoplifting. The officer said he was sure Bill was crying out for help. He recommended a therapist."

Dick shook his head. "We don't need a therapist."

"Well then, a marriage counselor."

He put his arms around me. "There is nothing wrong with us. I love you. Our marriage is perfect. It's the boys who are in trouble."

But I knew differently. Dick and I needed help. A family is a delicate mechanism, similar in its construction to a cobweb. When one area of the web is disturbed, all can sense it. We were that cobweb, all affected each other, and had been affected by the families that had preceded us. We were a modern nuclear family, living the suburban corporate life, which was so much the American way of the '50s and '60s.

We do not grow up in vacuums, and we bring into this world a history recorded in our genes as well as our surroundings. Nature and nurture are both vital factors in determining the "what" and "how" we shall be. I had developed the philosophy that raising children was like holding a peeled grape; one had to hold tight enough not to lose it, but not so tight that you had juice. I had gotten wise counsel, for as I had left the hospital to take my first child home, my doctor had said, "He was born independently of you. Allow him to remain so." With each child I tried to remember that, but it was difficult. The bond between parent and child is so intimate that the distinctions can become blurred. I struggled to make sure my children did not become extensions of my own ego.

I longed for authenticity in my relationship with my husband. But I was a novice in this business of marriage. I knew little about communication skills. I had never heard my parents argue. Not once. I had been on the debate team in high school and had learned methods of persuasion, but none of that ever seemed to apply to personal relationships. Dick and I never argued. We were always polite to each other. But we never had serious conversations. I could not get a "rise" out of Dick, get him to talk about anything unpleasant. We'd both grown up with the mantra *if you can't say something nice don't say anything at all*. We were in serious trouble.

Dick had inherited the disease of alcoholism. I didn't have a clue about what to do about his drinking, so did nothing. The first ten years of our marriage had been like a honeymoon. Dick was thoughtful and had a great sense of humor. During those early years, he was gone all week for his work. He earned the living. I took care of the house and children. A satisfactory arrangement. He never drank at home in the early days. However, by the time Bill was a teenager, Dick was at home more, drinking and blacking out daily. I began to feel I was living with a stranger.

Blackouts are terrifying and deadly. The drinker is still conscious, can still function—talk, drive the car—but the following day has no memory of what happened. None. Even when prompted, he is unable to recall anything. It's an amnesia-like experience. This must have terrified Dick and he could tell no one. He'd been an altar boy, Eagle Scout, and a Marine in World War II. In his culture, strong men never admitted to a weakness of this nature.

Now, most evenings, John and Mary were out with school activities. Bill and Doug were at home, their father in his red leather chair with his six-pack, usually passed out by ten. At that time, I knew nothing of the self-help group Alanon. It's a twelve-step program for individuals who have a loved one or friend who is alcoholic. I, like Dick, had always taken care of myself. People came to me with their problems, not the other way around. Although we led

11

a very social life, moving as often as we did made it difficult to establish deep friendships. To the world we presented a picture of a well-adjusted happy family, but these incidents with Bill screamed out that we were in serious trouble. Bill, it seemed, was our family's litmus test.

So I found a family counselor. He met with both Bill and Doug and said there was nothing wrong with them, just adolescent angst. He recommended strongly that Dick and I get some help. Only once did Dick go to a counseling session with me. I watched in amazement as the counselor did everything he could to get a response or an argument from Dick, but nothing worked. So I went to the sessions alone. I could sense relief in the children when I told them I was going to see a counselor on a weekly basis. I had no idea of the depth of denial I had been living in.

After my third session with the counselor, I went to Dick. "You've got to tell me when I do something you don't like, or when you're upset about something."

Again, he took me in his arms. "You're perfect and I love you," he said. "Stop this worrying."

Every week, the counselor asked me why I was working outside of the home. This was 1966 and the feminine revolution had not yet taken hold in my generation. None of my friends worked outside of their homes. Every week I had provided a new answer. I had lived in Atlanta when it was still a segregated city. What I saw there had led me to be deeply involved in the civil rights movement. I was an active "do-gooder," and the teaching helped answer some of that need. I'd been involved in activities all my life—burning the candle at both ends was something I thought I did well. No matter where the counselor probed, regardless of what he suggested, I came up with a clever response.

Dick was out of town the week of my fifth counseling session. This time the counselor boldly suggested that perhaps I was working because my marriage was not satisfactory to me. I was stunned at the thought.

I drove home in a mental fog. Wasn't this all I had ever wanted, to be married to a wonderful man and have children? Dick was a great provider and we loved one another. What had happened to us? I thought back to our first meeting. My parents had moved to Shorewood, a suburb of Milwaukee, during my senior year at college in Minneapolis, Minnesota. On graduating, I took a teaching job in Fond du Lac, Wisconsin. Each weekend I took the train to Milwaukee to visit my parents and enjoy my mother's marvelous cooking. On September the thirteenth, a Friday, my sister's boyfriend arranged a blind date for me. We were to meet the young man after a high school football game. During the game half, my sister, her boyfriend, and I walked past the bleachers. Out of the corner of my eye, I saw a handsome fellow wearing a camel hair sport jacket and red tie. My sister and her date stopped and this fellow came over and began to talk to me. I looked up at him and with as much sarcasm as I could muster said, "I don't believe we've met," and walked away. The fellow turned to my sister's date and said, "That's the girl I'm going to marry." And marry me he did. My mother described our courtship as "a romance like reading it out of a story book."

These memories flooded my mind as I parked the car in the garage. I went upstairs, spoke to no one, went into my bedroom, and threw myself across the bed. I didn't cry, couldn't, but a cold feeling paralyzed my body. Would there be no happy ending to this romance?

At one point I heard the children whispering in the hall. Apparently the automatic oven had gone on and dinner was cooking. I heard them later, as if from far away, when dinner was ready. I couldn't move. I thought how unprepared I was, we both were, for marriage and family. We had no manual, no guidebook, not even others to give us good advice. We weren't slackers, but were conscientious, bright people and had been doing the best we could. What had happened?

The house became quiet. I never closed my eyes, didn't shed a tear, but finally roused. It was 5:00 in the morning! I was stunned. I got up and wandered through the house feeling in the depths of my heart that my marriage was dead. The children were all asleep, the dishes had been done, the house was tidy. My dreams of a family with a father playing with his children and a mother overseeing a happy home had ended. I had to face the facts that my husband was an alcoholic and deeply troubled, and that I had a raft of problems of my own.

I again wondered what could possibly have happened to Bill, and picked up a family picture on my desk. We had been corporate gypsies, going wherever the large corporation my husband worked for sent us.

When Bill was in eighth grade, we moved to the San Francisco area. It was there I found Alanon and attended meetings. And after eighteen months, we were again transferred. John and Mary stayed behind, John at the San Francisco Art Institute, Mary working and sharing an apartment in San Mateo with a girlfriend.

Our transfer took us to Los Angeles. Dick was given an important position and his office was in Hollywood. We chose to live in Glendale so he could avoid a long commute on the freeways. I was concerned about this move, my sons' seventh, for I knew both Doug and Bill had suffered a cultural shock. The long hair so acceptable in their school in the Bay area was definitely taboo in the conservative atmosphere of Glendale. I wondered about their making new friends, but they assured me it was "taken care of."

I was amazed. "So quickly?" I asked.

They smiled. "Bill's got a plan," was all Doug would say.

His plan worked well. Every day at lunchtime they met in the outdoor cafeteria area and sat on a bench, the same bench every day. Then they laughed and talked with each other, enjoying their own company. It didn't take long. Soon one person joined them and then another. Before long, they had their own network of friends. "No sweat," Bill said. He never had a problem having friends, and he didn't seem to care.

Doug often joined me in the kitchen as I made dinner. He sat with his fanny draped in the sink, his long legs dangling. I loved these conversations. One afternoon he said he and Bill had been talking. (The boys were still at home, attending high school) Doug wanted me to know they would be fine when I divorced their dad.

I was shocked. "Divorce! Your father and I never even argue. We love each other."

"Mom," Doug said. "You can't stay." He put his hands together and moved them up. Then he continued moving one. "Dad's stuck here, but you've moved on. Bill and I will live with you and we can work part-time." My sons could see the end of the marriage in sight.

It took me three years to go, but I was able to leave my marriage cleanly and thank Dick for supporting us all the years we had together. I couldn't afford a lawyer and so bought a do-it-yourself divorce kit and went into the courtroom alone. My sister and her husband disapproved and it took two years before they forgave me and spoke to me. My parents lived two hours away and figured I'd handle it alone. I told my children not to come, for it would mean airplane tickets John and Mary could ill afford, and I didn't want Bill and Doug to miss school. I think I felt so guilty about getting a divorce—the first in either of our families—that I figured I couldn't ask for any support. And so I sat in the courtroom alone, scared to death. I heard a noise and looked up to see my dear friend Judy sliding in beside me. "I didn't think you should be alone today," she said. I was moved to tears by her thoughtful gesture.

My friends found a small apartment in Pasadena for me and I moved in. I had not asked for alimony and my final settlement was less than $5000, not enough to do much with, so I went to Europe for a month's visit with friends and relatives. It would take some time and a lot of work to get *myself* back.

My heart ached for those two young people who had fallen in love, married, and had four children. We had been so full of hope, so innocent. What had happened, I wondered? A friend who went to an all-male Alanon meeting said his heart broke at how helpless they all were. "We're like beached whales," he said.

An unfamiliar feeling of panic hit me as I returned the picture to my desk.

Chapter Three

All of these thoughts of Bill rattled around in my head as I waited for a call. I had to talk to someone. Instinctively I called Albert, a young Anglican priest the age of my youngest son, Doug, and dear to me.

"Hello, Luv." The lilt of his Irish voice carried his smile. "How are you?" We were interrupted by a call on the other line and I asked him to hold.

That Thursday morning, Doug had called Bill at his office, something he had never done before. Bill wasn't there, so Doug talked with Terry, Bill's boss. Terry felt a close connection with Bill. Some months earlier, Terry had been depressed. It was Bill who had come to him, made him shower and dress, and taken him to work. Bill was the one who had written the brilliant organizational plan for the company, getting them generous raises in the process. Their relationship had grown to one of mutual respect. Terry was convinced that Bill had been in an accident and was lying unconscious somewhere. Bill would never do anything rash. He was too responsible, too conscientious.

Doug called Laura. "There's something funny going on," she said. Doug heard her concern and so contacted her throughout the day. Shortly after 2:00 in the afternoon, Laura called Doug. Her voice was panicky as she told him she'd gotten a letter from Bill. Doug said he'd come right away and told her to call Terry.

As Doug drove to Laura's, a feeling of fear triggered in him. He gripped the steering wheel, knuckles white, as he pleaded out loud over and over, "Bill, don't do this." Terry soon arrived. They read the letter, and Doug called the police station and told them about it. The officer told them to come to the station to file a missing person report. The three of them piled into the car and went to the police station. An officer asked them to wait in an interview room and left.

I pressed the "flash" button. My son Doug was the caller. I told him I was talking to Albert on the other line. Doug's tone was like that of a loving parent with a frightened child. "Mom," his voice gentle but firm, "Tell Albert you'll call him right back. And tell him to wait. It's important."

I felt my body go on alert. Albert said he'd wait for my call.

Doug then told me he was at the police station. He said the detective had taken him aside and said they had a "John Doe" who fit the description of Bill.

I gripped the phone trying to understand what Doug was telling me. *A John Doe,* I thought. *What's that?* My mind struggled frantically to make sense out of what he was saying. And I felt my body steel itself against a shock it feared might come. "And Laura?" I asked.

"Terry's taking her home. Her mom's there. And they'll call Bill's friends Sandy and Donna." He paused. "Mom," his voice again gentle but firm. "Call Albert, Mom, and tell him to come be with you. Don't be alone. I've called John and he's coming, but it will take a while. Albert's closer."

I listened unable to fully comprehend what was happening. "Mom," Doug said. "Call Albert. Okay?"

I called Albert and mechanically told him what Doug had said. His response was immediate. "I'll be right there, Luv. Wait for me."

Death never entered my mind. I've had little to do with death. My grandparents had all died and my parents had traveled to their funerals, leaving my sister and me behind with baby-sitters. I had attended only two funerals in my whole life, and those of people I knew only slightly.

I'd had two babies die in utero, but I'd never held them in my arms or heard them cry. The doctors took care of everything and I was too ill to protest. When I wept, my mother scolded, "Don't cry." How dare I cry?

"Stiff upper lip," my father had said. "Be brave." I was always being told to be brave. I knew my parents believed it was the wisest and most loving thing to say. I also knew their personal experience with death was almost as limited as mine. Death was never discussed. Not one of us had seen someone die. We hardly talked about illness, let alone dying.

My husband Dick had been a Marine in the South Pacific during World War II. He knew about death and dying first hand, but he never talked about it. Not once did I ever hear him refer to any of the dread of that war. To my questions about it he smiled and said it was over and best forgotten. All the fears of that handsome young man facing mortal combat were locked up inside of him.

I must have discussed death with my children, for we'd had a menagerie of animals through the years. Our funny bouncy Sebastian (a Puli puppy) was stolen and we all cried at the loss. But we soon bought another wonderful dog. When our precious Siamese cat was hit by a car, the children and I took her to our vet. We waited patiently while he examined her. No one moved or said a word when he walked into the lobby. "I'm sorry," he said. "We couldn't save her." I gathered the children in my arms and we wept together. That evening we told my husband and held him while he cried. We soon had another beautiful Siamese cat. The death of animals, although it tore at our hearts, was expected. But people? That was something we had no experience with.

It was Bill, this son who was now late to work and had sent a letter to his wife, who had maintained a cemetery in the back yard while he was growing up. Birds, mice, fish, baby alligators, and garter snakes made up the majority of the little graves. Each was a small mound, with a cross, some with names carefully burned into the wood. I often saw him on his knees tending the little graves. We had never taken the children to a real cemetery, not out of denial, but because we lived a nuclear existence, thousands of miles from parents and relatives. I have never seen my maternal grandparents' graves and only saw my paternal grandparents' graves a few years ago. Neither one of my parents wanted a grave. They asked that their ashes be scattered in the ocean.

We were a healthy family and death was a stranger to us. The only grave my children ever visited was that of John Kennedy. He had been their president, the first they had really noticed. It was misting the day we were there, and so there were few tourists. We all stood silently for a long time before the flame, not hiding our tears. No one spoke on the drive back to our hotel.

After my father entered a nursing home we all visited him regularly. Bill and Laura made a point of going often, taking their children, telling stories about their adventures and giving him "wheelies" in his wheelchair.

My father refused to say the words "die" or "death." As he approached his own dying (at age 90), I asked if he wanted to talk about it. He gave me a piercing look to be sure the conversation was not just idle talk. I was sincere. I knew Mother could never have this conversation. I was the elder daughter and felt a responsibility for my father's welfare. Mother had always used me as the "communicator," reminding me to tell Daddy when her birthday was due, or bring up a touchy subject she was afraid to broach. I also knew how valuable it was to be sure we had no undelivered communications in our relationship; to be sure we said all that needed to be said. This wisdom had not been available to me in my marriage, and Dick and I had both suffered as a result. Neither one of us knew how to have those "difficult" conversations where the truth is exposed. They stayed buried, stifling our love, causing a chasm to grow between us. I did not want that happening any more. I wanted to be a safe space into which my father could express himself honestly. "Let's talk," I said. "One of those honest person to person talks about dying."

He smiled, his blue eyes so alive in his frail body. "No need to talk," he said. "We all kick the bucket." He winked at me. That was his reference to death. He would "kick the bucket."

I drove home from that visit with my father deep in thought. "Kick the bucket" was an expression that came from hangings. A person was strung up by a rope and made to stand on an overturned bucket. Someone then kicked the bucket, and the person was hanged. So death would come and "kick the bucket" upon which my father stood and he would die.

My father's body and mind were failing rapidly. "He never complains," my mother said. She laughed and said, "I complain all the time." My mother visited him every day, eating lunch with him, and wheeling him about the halls and gardens. They were Nonnie and Boppie to everyone, names my son John (their first grandchild) had given them when he was small, names that had stuck. Everyone in the nursing home knew them. My mother, so sweet and gentle, her white hair piled into a soft knot at the back of her head, always knitting, making hats and scarves for great grandchildren, needlework tree ornaments for the hospital, bringing my father his favorite whole wheat chocolate chip cookies, and sneaking in wine for his daily aperitif.

My father, always involved in some project or other, had ridden his horse daily until in his late 80s. "You're too old to be riding," his doctor had finally insisted. "So's the horse," was my father's reply. But now his legs no longer supported him and the tiny blood vessels in his brain were sabotaging him at a rapid rate. It broke my heart to see him struggle to find the words he wanted to say. I knew he was ready to die.

"How are you doing?" I had asked on my next weekly visit.

"Can't seem to check out of life," he said. As if it were a hotel he was ready to leave.

"Why don't you just go?" I whispered.

"I keep trying," he replied. "But I keep not going. Why, when you're ready, can't you just go?"

My father, at the end of long life, wanted to go and couldn't. He was actually welcoming death.

Like a dutiful child I waited for Albert to come. I paced through my house, every cell in my body steeled against the possibility of death. I felt like a tightrope walker, every muscle holding me upright on a thread. I called upon God and all the powers of the universe to hear a mother's plea. He's not dead. Not dead. No! If I could deny it strongly enough, not admit it was so, it might go away. I implored God with all of the strength I had to have it not be true, as if by sheer will alone I could stop the hand of fate.

I looked at the picture of Laura and Bill on the long table behind the sofa. Laura, dark eyes laughing, her face full of joy. Bill, so strikingly handsome, trying to hold his grin in check. Not injured. Not dead, this vital alive man who always keeps his word and gets things done. Not my son who had entered life so vigorously, who'd survived all the traumas of being a teen-ager in the 60s, who was so caring and spiritual, who was making his way so well in life. Oh no, not dead.

I thought again of the letter Bill had sent to Laura. Was he leaving her? But why send a letter? That didn't make sense. But a strange fear began to build in the back of my mind.

The detective took Doug to the parking lot in Santa Monica where Bill's car was parked. It was surrounded by yellow crime scene tape. "This is an investigation," the detective said. "Don't touch anything."

Bill had parked his car so he could look into the window of the hospital where his two sons had been born. The elderly parking attendant who had often seen Bill was weeping. He was sure Bill had had a heart attack. "He was such a gentleman," he said. "Always so nice. So kind to me." He patted Doug's back. "I'm so sorry."

Bill was composed, holding the steering wheel, the car keys in his hand. He was sitting upright, his eyes closed. His head was tilted forward, as if he had merely fallen asleep. Doug stood, silently looking at the body of his brother. These brothers were only fourteen months apart in age and had been good friends. The detective asked Doug if he could identify the body.

There was no doubt. It was Bill. Doug squatted down so he could see squarely into Bill's face. He looked until he realized his brother was no longer there, only the body that had housed him. As Doug stood, he noticed the bottle of organic fruit juice on the floor. Beside it was a small pharmaceutical bottle, the poison that had carried the lethal dose. *Just like Bill*, Doug thought. It was clear Bill didn't want there to be any mystery about what had happened. Even in dying he would be true to himself.

Doug's gestures spoke loudly of his love for his brother and family. He returned to the police station and filled out the necessary paperwork. Then he went to Laura's home to tell her. This news was too important for the phone.

When Albert finally arrived at my home, I was calm. "Would you like a cup of tea?" I asked.

Albert, familiar with death and dying, took my shoulders and gently shook me. "Let go, Ruth. Let go." He then hugged me and I felt the tug of tears in my eyes. But I could not let my defenses go. If I could just deny death strongly enough, it would not be so.

We sat on the sofa, he held my hands and we talked. I have no recollection of what I said, I only know he listened intently. As long as I could talk about Bill, perhaps I could fool Death. Something would happen and I would hear it was all a big mistake. Miracles could and did happen.

My phone rang and Albert and I rushed to get it. It was Laura. "Oh, Ruth," she sobbed. "Bill's dead. He was your son. I'm so sorry for you—for us. I loved him so."

Albert held me, and the three of us sobbed together. My son was dead. The deed was done and by his own hand.

Chapter Four

Like a bomb, Laura's words exploded at my very center. I lost all sense of who I was. I wanted to die. Why live, I wondered. What's the point? I envied those women who scream, pound their breasts, and rend their clothes. My grief was tearing me apart, my tears like molten lava in my throat. I felt frozen, numb, as if I too had died.

I asked Laura if she wanted me to come to be with her. "No," she said, "I think I need to be alone with the boys." Her two small sons, Bill's beloved boys, were just four and two. I wasn't sure she should be alone, but was too numb to argue.

This man, my son, was dead. I could hardly think the thought. He'd been born curious about life, had never been afraid to stand up for his beliefs, even when very young. It was scary for me as his mother as he seemed to have no fear. He had an inner confidence and strength that was a threat to some and a fascination to others. He seemed to glow from within while at the same time there was a darkness in him I had never been able to fathom.

To lose a loved one to death is painful. To have that loved one choose to die, deliberately do what it takes to end life, is excruciating. The news of his death had a physical impact. It struck deep into my heart; a mortal blow from which I feared I would never fully recover. And the blow was to my entire body, not just my mind. It's as if my mind said, *if you let this information in you will surely die.* And so my body steeled itself against the trauma.

We are never ready for death, even when we see it approaching, when we know it will bring peace and the end of suffering. Even when we are prepared, death is a shock. When that death is of your child, it goes against all the rules of nature.

Author Carlos Castaneda's mentor, a Yaqui medicine man from Sonora, says that a child's birth leaves a hole in that luminous egg which we are, a hole that can never be closed, where we are forever vulnerable.

It's as if the world is a luminous egg and when someone dies, life is taken from that world. I felt as if life had been ripped from my body. The fabric of my life had been shattered. My life would not be restructured in the same way. It couldn't be, for the mark of death is permanent.

Now there were two words I would have to deal with. Not the words *per se*, but the concepts and thinking behind them. The first was "never" and the other "why."

Never is an absolute. Not ever; at no time; by no chance; in no case; under no conditions. Never to see him again. Never to talk with him again. Never to hear his laugh, his voice on the phone, his "Hi, what's happening?" Never.

Some friends spoke of resurrection. Others talked of karma and reincarnation. All meant to comfort me, as if skipping over the "dead" phase would make it easier. But I knew that in order to heal I had to face death in all its absoluteness and, hopefully someday, accept the "never." I was terrified.

They say before dying, one's life passes before one's eyes. I thought of my son's life, looking to see what could have gone wrong. Had I made some dreadful mistakes? I knew I had not been a perfect mother. True, my major in college had been child welfare, but when my children were born I threw away the manuals and followed my heart the best way I knew how.

Bill had not been an easy child. The experience I'd gained raising John and Mary was of no use with this little boy. He was beautiful, sturdy, sure of himself, feared nothing, and had a stubborn will of his own. Maybe we'd made him grow up too soon, deprived him of his babyhood. He gave up napping before he was two, so I used Doug's naptime to read to him. It gave us a chance to be together. I always had a pile of picture books, but Bill typically made his own choice. He didn't want to read those baby books. He wanted to read books like I read, so he picked out a beat-up copy of *Kim* that my grandparents had given me. We curled up on the couch and I read to him. "Oh, ye who tread the Narrow Way, By Toiphet-flare to Judgment Day, Be gentle when the heathen pray To Buddha at Kamakura."[1] Kipling's words, like a river, flowed over Bill way beyond his grasp. He chose the book every day. I only hoped someday he'd grow up into the words.

When Bill was three, I sent him to a day camp that met two mornings a week. Bill hated it. I thought back to those days when I made him go. He

---

[1]   Kipling, p. 1

always cried, and I was filled with guilt. Was it then he started having those strange quiet spells that plagued him all his life?

Bill always longed to be older, more able. He posed for pictures pretending to be grown-up. He used his eating utensils with a flourish, usually spilling food as he did so. He always seemed so sure of himself. Not cocky, just sure. Some people had a problem with that. I know my mother did.

Bill was six when we moved to the city where my parents were living. This was his fourth move. My mother loved having us come for Sunday dinner. Occasionally the children spent an overnight. They liked going. Daddy let them make boats out of wood and nails. Mother read her cookbooks to them, adding silly ingredients. Though loving with the others, my mother was distant with Bill. It became so noticeable that Mary and John commented on it. Finally Doug (almost five) protested. Bill never complained, but then he never complained about anything.

I finally spoke to her. "What is it about Bill?" I asked. "Is he misbehaving?"

She shook her head. "No . . . He's just not as cuddly as the others, so cool, kind of distant."

How interesting, I thought, for my mother was like that, distant and reserved. I knew my mother loved me, but I can't remember her holding me or kissing me. Daddy was different, hugging and teasing all the time. He called Mary his little "snuggle bunny" and wiggled his ears for the boys. Mother was one cool cookie.

"If you can't treat Bill like the others, I can't come anymore," I said.

Mother cried.

"She's right," Daddy said. "We've got to love them all equally."

I'll give Mother credit. She opened her heart to Bill and he responded in kind. He never said anything, but he made special drawings for her, as if he sensed her need for love and approval.

Many years later I realized my mother suffered from bouts of depression. We didn't have a name for it then, but I remember how quiet the house was during those long winter months in central Wisconsin when I was a girl. She had a wicked sense of humor and could be so funny. But she also suffered from a kind of anemia that left her devoid of energy. She was always busy, but I think the toll on her mood was great.

I thought about how quiet Bill had always been. He wasn't a talker, never had been. I could not remember his ever telling how he felt about anything, even when he was little. He never complained, not because he was virtuous, but because I don't think he could. I know I had lectured the children about being respectful and not calling each other bad names, but I think Bill's refusal went beyond that. I don't think he was *able* to talk about how he felt. My other children talked with me and told me, well, not everything, but most of what was going on in their lives. They had no trouble telling me "bad" things. What was it about Bill that made communicating so difficult?

During his early teenage years, he seemed rather flat. I had not a clue as to what was happening in his relationship with his father. On the surface it seemed cold and distant, but Dick was like that with all the children by then. During those teenage years whenever I returned from an Alanon meeting, I checked with the boys. Doug always told me what had happened that evening with their father. When I went to Bill's room he always said, "It's cool. I'm okay." He never told me anything about his father's verbal abuse.

He definitely had trouble talking about himself, but his actions shouted loudly how he felt. Our whole family is a little like that. I can relate to those English movies and novels—you know, "stiff upper lip and all that." Those virtues were in the very air my husband and I breathed as children. We both grew up in a code of silence. There had been a great depression and a world war. People had no time for minor complaints or tears. Products of our history, culture, and choices, I shuddered to think that my quiet husband and I had instilled this attitude in our children.

My heart ached as I desperately tried to figure out what could have driven my son to do this desperate act. I felt as if a giant Samurai sword had split me down the middle and wondered if I could survive this pain. Instinctively I knew that the daily routines and rituals of living would bring us needed healing. But first we needed to allow ourselves to be deeply wounded. I was numb, as if wrapped in cotton batting. I had to deal with the raw gaping wound of having my son's life taken from us.

Any death is a cause to mourn, but when the death is a suicide, the grief is compounded. The elements of anger, shock, and guilt present in any death are now magnified and must be dealt with. But later. Now we needed to be treated like patients in intensive care. We would take care of each other, gently and lovingly. Our humble attempts communicated love loudly. I found relief and comfort in that love.

Chapter Five

After identifying his brother's body, Doug called John and told him of Bill's suicide. John said he'd come to me right away. Although Doug stood taller, John was the "Big Bruddah" to his "Little Bruddah." John's hair, now silvery white, had begun to gray while he was in his early thirties and it made his blue eyes sparkle. A natural at athletics, John had played hockey up through semi-pro, had been a gymnast, played guitar in a group, and was an artist. He had worked primarily as an art director for publications and now worked successfully in the film industry.

My husband Dick had traveled for most of John's growing-up years, so John had taken seriously his role as big brother and protector. When he was just four, he'd come into the kitchen, little pop-gun in hand. "I'm going out to kill all the bears," he'd say. I'd fill his pockets with raisins and graham crackers and he'd leave. When his pockets were empty, he'd return. "Well, dear," he'd report, "I killed all the bears. You're safe now." He could be depended on to check up on us, and to make sure we were all in touch.

John arrived at my home, pale in his denial of the death. He could not, would not believe that Bill was dead. "Not Bill. He's not the kind to do anything like that. He's the one we all turned to. I can't believe it. If only I'd called him," he said. "If only I'd known." It was like a litany as he said it over and over. Then he turned to me. Gently he asked, "Does Mary know?"

My only daughter Mary, so strong in her quiet way, was married to tall Brent and the mother of five children. I adored her. I wanted to be the one to tell her. As I picked up the phone for the call, I thought of the kind of quiet courage Mary has always shown. I remembered when she was eight. I told her she had to take piano lessons.

"But I want to ride horses," she said.

"You've got to give the piano a try," I insisted. "At least for a year."

She practiced faithfully, and played in the recital. Bill and Doug, then just five and four, sat in little chairs in the front row and dramatically plugged their ears as she began the familiar tune she had learned. The recital was a success. As we drove up to our house she said, "It's been a year. Now can I ride horses?" She did, and won ribbons.

After her graduation from high school, I flew back to pick her up. She and her friends greeted me at the airport like a celebrity. On the flight back home, I asked her where she wanted to go to college. She looked at me and said, "Mom, I'm not yet ready to leave home. When I am, I'll let you know." She was like that. Really knew who she was.

"I'll call her," I told John. The call to Wisconsin went through, and Sarah, Mary's youngest, answered the phone.

"Is Daddy there?" I asked.

Sarah said, "Yes, but I've something important to tell you."

I lifted my heavy heart, and tried to sound interested. "What is it, dear?" She talked of a birthday party at a friend's. I heard her call for her father. Then she said, "I have more to tell you, Grammy. I love you, and I've lost another tooth."

Brent took the phone. "What's up? Mary's right here."

"Brent, I have some bad news to tell Mary. I want you to know first so you can be there for her. Bill has committed suicide."

He gasped. "Oh no. I can't believe it. No!"

I could hear Mary in the background, her voice breaking. "What is it?" She took the phone. "Mom, Mom, what's wrong?"

I told her, and we wept together, Brent and Sarah holding Mary in her grief, John and Albert supporting me.

"We'll come right away," Mary said. "We'll be there."

They gathered their family together that night, and talked about the death. Suicide. The word can hardly be spoken, and yet it was a reality for their family. They said a prayer for Bill, and for his family, his small sons and wife, and for all who were left behind.

"You need to call Nonnie," John said.

I dreaded making that call to my mother. As I walked to my desk, the phone rang. It was my mother. I was stunned. It was like ESP. She never called me—never. I always made the calls. She started to talk about a problem, and I interrupted her. "Mother, I want you to sit down as I have some bad news."

"I am sitting. What is it?"

I told her of Bill's suicide.

I heard her gasp. "Not our Bill," she said. "He's so responsible, so dependable. We brag about him to everyone. Oh no. I won't tell your father. It would kill him."

Too weak to even engage in a conversation, I told her to do what she thought best.

Doug finally arrived at my home. "Where is he?" I asked.

Doug took my hand. "They need to perform an autopsy as it is an unnatural death."

"Oh," I cried. "Don't let them hurt him."

Doug hugged me and promised they would not.

My friend Patrick had planned to come from Phoenix to visit that weekend. I called him, told him what had happened, and gave him a choice to come or not. He chose to come, as he knew I would need him. "Are you all right?" he asked. I had no idea, for I could feel nothing. "Just hang on," he said. "I'll be there."

"You can't be alone tonight," Doug said. "Call Aunt Mary."

I called my sister and asked her to spend the night with me. She agreed to come.

Albert knew a way to allow us to begin to deal with the reality of Bill's suicide. He held my arms tightly and looked me in the eye. "We'll have a Eucharist," he said. "Just you and your family, in the chapel at 8:30 tomorrow morning. I'll see you there." His intensity penetrated the fog around me, and I agreed. "You know what to do, Ruth," he said. "And you'll do it."

My sister Mary Ann finally arrived. Doug asked her what had taken her so long. She said she kept putting off leaving her house, for she knew that when she saw me she would have to acknowledge it was really so, that Bill had committed suicide.

"Have you had dinner?" she asked me.

I shook my head.

"Well," she said, "I'm hungry and you need to eat." She drove us to a gourmet Chinese restaurant. The food was like straw in my mouth. I was numb, more dead than alive.

Chapter Six

That evening of my son's death I went into my office, and opened the package from my daughter. She knew I was writing children's books and stories. Her note read, "I don't know if you have read this. If not, it's great. I hope you enjoy it. Love, Mary." It was a little children's book, *Love You Forever* by Robert Munsch. There are no accidents, no coincidences. I took the little book with me to read in bed.

Through Erhard's est Training I had learned how vital it is to experience our lives. It's a simple process. You merely have to be conscious, pay attention, and notice the sensations in your body. Then just let them be, and they will complete and drain away.

I was locked in the denial I'd first experienced hearing Bill had not shown up at work. Then the trauma of hearing of his death had struck its mortal blow. My body and mind were in a frozen, coma-like state. I needed to be fully conscious if I was going to get through this and be of help to my loved ones. The Dead Sea is dead because it has no outlet. I needed to deal with my feelings.

I understood all of this, but it was of little use at this stage. Understanding did nothing to lessen the pain. I understand that a knife is sharp and can cut my finger. I even understand how my nervous system relays its messages to my brain, and why and how the body goes into denial at a time of trauma. I understand all of that, but it does nothing to ease the hurt. It was my pain I needed to deal with.

I was actually afraid to experience the feelings for fear they'd kill me. Feelings are real. They are in our bodies. The words we use to describe how we are feeling are the labels that name the emotions. You don't "feel" fear. You feel a tightness in your stomach, body sensations. Those sensations, along with your thoughts, have you name the emotion. That pounding in your heart, shortness of breath, and sweaty brow can be the passion of love or anger. You are the decider.

I didn't need to name my body sensations. I needed to experience them and not talk about them. Until you consciously experience these sensations, they remain hidden in your body.

I knew from my research in learning theory that our memories are not stored some place in the brain like recorded film. More likely they are all over the place in our neurological systems. More than once I'd heard someone tell of having a long forgotten memory evoked during a rolfing session or deep massage.

But now this "knowing" was all academic and of no use to me in my pain at the death of my son. I knew I needed to begin to experience what was going on for me.

I was terrified to face the full reality of Bill's death, to let my grief surface. I don't like pain and am not masochistic. As I was growing up, I learned that one of the worst things I could do, according to my father, was to cry. "If you cry," he'd say, "you'll have to go to your room." I'd spent a lifetime managing to keep my emotions well in check. Now I actually feared I might "go off the deep end" and fall apart. However, at some deep level I knew I had to let the pain in, and so I opened the little book and began to read.

It begins with a young mother who holds her newborn son and looks at him lovingly. Softly she sings to him:

> *I'll love you forever,*
> *I'll like you for always,*
> *As long as I'm living*
> *my baby you'll be.* [2]

I recalled seeing this beautiful baby, Bill, right after his birth. Secretly, I had said I would have four children before I was thirty. John and Mary were eighteen months apart. I again conceived a baby that would have been eighteen months younger than Mary. One morning, in the sixth month of the pregnancy, I realized I had not felt the baby move for some time and called the doctor. The baby was dead. When I finally returned home from the hospital, my mother and mother-in-law both were surprised at my grief

---

[2]   Munsch

at the loss. They had lived during the depression when another baby might mean the difference between having food on the table or not. The doctor said I was to wait a year before attempting another pregnancy. I had waited and here was this beautiful child.

I continued reading the picture book. It told of the baby's growth until he was two, trashing the house, driving the mother to say, "This kid is driving me crazy!"[3] I remembered Bill's independence at that age. John brought chicken pox home from kindergarten. He and Mary had mild cases, but Bill's eyes were scabbed shut, his little bottom covered with ugly scabs. When I described this to the pediatrician, he became so concerned that he came out to the house. As the doctor walked into the living room, Bill wandered in, dragging his gun and holster behind him. He wanted to play. The doctor was stunned, and dropped into a chair. With tears in his eyes he told me it was the second worst case of chicken pox he'd ever seen. "The worst was when I was a resident at Bellevue in New York," he'd said. "That patient died."

Bill had not been easy to raise. When he was older, one of his favorite pictures was taken when he was not yet two years old. I am walking around the corner of the house into the backyard carrying Bill. He is crying and the look on my face is easy to read. I'm angry. He had pleaded with me to go into the backyard to play with John and Mary. I had relented as he promised faithfully to stay in the backyard. But he didn't. He wouldn't. He was too independent. His first phrase was, "I do it." He was curious about everything and feared nothing.

Bill wasn't mean. He was sweet, very quiet, and extremely thoughtful. But he was stubborn with a will of his own. In the late afternoons during those early years, while I was preparing dinner, John and Mary watched "The Mickey Mouse Club." Daily, Bill sidled up to the TV set, quickly turned it off, and ran down the hallway, with Mary and John in hot pursuit. Bill thought it a great game. John would lug Bill into the kitchen. "Can't you do something with this kid?"

I finally hired Monty, the teenager from across the street, to take Bill for a ride in the wagon, so John and Mary could watch their only TV show for the day, and I could cook in peace. Our housing development was new, no sidewalks or roads, and I watched in horror as Monty raced along the bumpy ruts with Bill bouncing about laughing.

---

³   Ibid.

Bill was only fourteen months old when Doug was born. He adored the baby, dumped his toys into Doug's crib, and fed him chocolate cookies stolen from my cache in the kitchen. He played with Doug, sitting on his little legs, leaning forward, shouting "Peek-a-boo!" Doug gasped then laughed until he was breathless. Gasp. Giggle. Breathe. It's a wonder those two had survived. But they did and became fast friends

I thought of Bill going to kindergarten. The children all walked to school and I wanted Bill to walk with John and Mary. But Bill was slow about getting dressed and coming to breakfast. I tried everything I could think of, which was mostly nagging. That got him to school on time, but left me feeling awful. So one day I told him I would wake him only once. He had to get dressed and come to breakfast on time all on his own. "If you're late, you'll have to walk alone and go see the principal," I told him. The next morning he showed up at the breakfast table dressed and ready for school right on time. I was impressed. He managed to be on time all week.

We lived then in a suburb of New York City and my husband's work often required that he stay in Manhattan to attend show openings and cocktail parties for celebrities his company represented. I didn't mind at all, for he always invited me to go with him. We usually got home long after the children were in bed. While Dick drove our baby sitter home, I went in and checked on the children. This particular evening I sat down on Bill's bed and hit something hard. I pulled back the bedding. There was Bill, in his pajamas, and underneath he was fully dressed, even his shoes! Typical of Bill, thinking "outside of the box."

The little boy in the picture book grew to be nine. At that age, Bill talked me into being a Den Mother. He loved scouting. The Father-Son Banquet was to be a special affair for him that year, as he was receiving several awards. He bathed, with no prompting from me, dressed, and sat in the living room, waiting for his father. Dinnertime came, but Bill refused to eat. He'd have his dinner at the banquet, he told me. I volunteered to take him, but he refused. "No," he said, "Dad's taking me." By seven o'clock I knew it was too late, but Bill stubbornly sat in the living room. Dick finally arrived, in no condition to go anywhere. I tried to cover up for him. "I think he's got the flu." Bill just gave me a "look" and went upstairs to his bedroom. He never mentioned the incident, but was quiet for days.

I had agreed to teach Sunday School to a group of teen-aged boys. It was a challenge, one I barely survived each week. One of the boys in the group (I'll call him James) was obviously ostracized by the others. I didn't know why and it troubled me. One evening at dinner, Mary told me James was in the hospital. He'd had nine hours of surgery, the final attempt to build an anus as he'd been born without one.

"Are you going to go visit him?" Mary asked.

I shuddered. I hate hospitals.

"You should go," nine-year-old Bill said. He got up from the table and took his dishes to the kitchen. "I'll go with you."

I felt trapped and knew I had to go. We were quiet on the drive to the hospital. The nurse was relieved to see us. There had been no other visitors. "Poor kid," she said. "His family doesn't seem to care."

James' room was dark and smelled strongly of antiseptics and medications. I had to breathe deeply to keep from getting light-headed. It looked like James was asleep with all manner of tubes and monitors about his body. As Bill and I sat there, I silently prayed for this boy I didn't know. After what I decided was a respectable time, I suggested we leave.

"Better say good-bye," Bill said.

I tiptoed to the bed. James was deathly white and looked at peace. I leaned over and kissed his forehead.

"Mrs. Maxwell," he whispered, "I knew you'd come."

Tears flooded my eyes. I felt terrible. Only at the prompting of my young son had I come, and then reluctantly had waited until I could get away. I looked carefully at my son, and longed for the kind of compassion he had demonstrated. On the ride home I thanked Bill for suggesting we come. "It's okay," he said, "I knew you should." The child leading the parent.

And then Bill became a teenager, like the boy in the picture book. That age is often difficult for kids. For Bill it was torture. He had gained weight, pre-puberty fat, and he hated it. I showed him a picture of his father at the same age. He had also looked pudgy, but had grown into a slim six-foot tall handsome man. I reminded Bill he'd lose the fat as he grew, but it made no difference. It was no consolation. His weight depressed him. I became concerned when he stopped eating breakfast so made hamburgers and hot chocolate to entice him. He nibbled politely.

And then we were transferred again. This would be my ninth move, Bill's sixth. We chose to live in Burlingame, outside of San Francisco. John lived in the city and attended the San Francisco Institute of Art. Mary was a freshman at a local college. Both Doug and Bill adjusted quickly to their new high school, but I was concerned about Bill. He was too quiet. I decided we needed to communicate and so I made an appointment for us to meet to do just that. We took glasses of iced tea out to the patio and settled ourselves under the pepper tree. "What do you want to talk about?" I asked.

He shrugged. "I dunno. What do you want to talk about?"

I struggled to find a subject we could discuss. For about fifteen minutes we "hemmed and hawed" at each other. It seemed hopeless and I finally gave up. As we walked to the house, Bill said, "What time shall we do this tomorrow?"

I was stunned. I thought it had been a failure. Bill had not. We met regularly for our little hemming and hawing sessions.

I have no memories of being worried about Doug. It was Bill I was concerned about. He was not only quiet, but seemed emotionally flat. One morning, while serving breakfast, I took the little sticky label from the bunch of bananas and stuck it on my nose. Bill laughed.

The next morning, I found it stuck to the window above the kitchen sink. We took turns with the little label until all the stickiness was gone. That Christmas, I opened a gift from Bill to find it in a small frame. Bill, creative and funny, but far too quiet.

The boy in the picture book grew up, as did my son, and his interests changed. We'd moved to the Los Angeles area and lived in Glendale. Bill began to seek for deep spiritual truths. I gave Bill an article from the *Los Angeles Times* about Maharishi Mahesh Yogi and Transcendental Meditation classes. Bill asked me to drive him to Beverly Hills so he could learn about TM. Now the untidy boy tossed aside his boyish interests and cleaned his room. He bought a narrow futon to sleep on, and took over his dad's old roll-top desk. My cousin's Chinese wife had given me lovely antique figurines. Bill asked for them, and placed them on his dresser. His bedroom now was a clean, clear space. He left clever notes for himself, reminding him of things he needed to do or remember. Little scraps of paper: "Be grateful;" "Stand erect;" "Marty's present;" "Happiness is within you;" "Peace of mind;" "TM meeting in Glendale;" "Don't waste your time;" "Wait—Think—Fast;" "Don't be negative + Be happy everything that exists is good." All were decorated with stars, planets, moons, and arrows. Bill was seriously embarked on a spiritual quest to improve himself. It looked like he had a clear internal model toward which he was working.

Bill now woke at five, meditated for an hour, did yoga for an hour, ate a vegetarian breakfast and went to school. He continued this practice and finally graduated high school.

Our next move was to Ventura, a small town on the Pacific coast north of Los Angeles. It was while living there that I finally asked my husband for a divorce.

I moved into Pasadena, where my closest friends lived. Bill and Doug, now nineteen and eighteen, were out on their own, working to provide for their living and schooling. I was unable to do so, and they refused to ask their father for help. I asked for no alimony so had to get out and scramble to earn my own living. My sons and their friends often gathered in my small apartment. We were like adventurous college students, laughing about our newfound poverty, and keeping our spirits up. I was torn between being proud of their strength and courage, and feeling badly that I couldn't do more for them.

And then, like the boy of the picture book, my son fell in love with a wonderful girl, married and had two sons of his own, sons he loved and cared for.

On each page of the little book, I grieved the loss of my baby. I wept for the child he'd been, the teenager, young man, and adult. I faced the void in my womb, a raw and gaping hurt. My arms ached to hold my son, and I felt a pain of such loss I had no words for it. I cried as I had never cried before in my life, my body convulsed in weeping. And scariest of all, I let my thoughts run, unedited. I allowed them to flow by like the music roll on a player piano, refusing to engage in conversation with any of them—as tempting as that was. I wanted desperately to explain, to reason, and to justify, to get myself off the hook. I wanted to tell how dear his father had been when we were younger, what a wonderful provider he'd been, how loving, thoughtful, and funny. I wanted to explain what a deadly disease alcoholism is, subtle and baffling. How it causes a gradual shift in personality, how the alcohol speaks and acts in cruel ways. And I wanted to tell how helpless I felt in the face of it. I pleaded for forgiveness for all my stupid, thoughtless acts. But there was no one to tell, and so, in the style of meditative sitting, I just let the emotions run by, experiencing the feelings attached to them. Some of them were awful: my rage at how Bill could have done such a thing. The most responsible person I had ever known, one of the most spiritual, had done the most irresponsible deed. I felt grief and guilt over my possible duplicity with the alcoholism. Memories of isolated incidences poured in. How cruel is time in that it only goes forward. How desperately I longed to call back those times of hurt and loss from my son's life, from all our lives. I looked at the thoughts and felt the feelings, but I kept none of them. As I had learned in the est Training, I just experienced them and let them go. Later, I said. I'll deal with that later. For the present, I would just feel. I let my tears come up from the depths, knowing they were not only releasing, but also healing. I was sure I would be faced with thoughts and feelings about my son and his death all my life, and knew I would deal with them in this same way, letting them be, experiencing them, but keeping myself always open, for only in that way could I stay alive.

I finally fell into an exhausted sleep and dreamed I'm in a dark forest. I see an opening in the distance shaped like the moon gates in China. The light in the opening is an iridescent yellow-white and I run for it. I know if I can get there, I can pull Bill back out, back to life. Just as I reach the opening, a huge orange-red metal wall drops down with a deafening clang. The third time I do this, I know I can't get him back. It's true. He is really dead. I wonder if I will be able to bear such grief. But I know I must in order to be a repository for my son's memory.

Chapter Seven

At six o'clock the following morning, the phone rang. It was Laura. "Oh, Ruth," she cried through tears, the pain evident in her voice. "Come, please come. We need you. Come. Please." I told her we were on our way to the Chapel for a quick Eucharist and then would come directly to her. I knew then and know today that it will never be over. We all will carry the scars from this wound forever.

The phone rang again. "Mom." It was my daughter, Mary. "We're at O'Hare in Chicago, but there's a terrible blizzard. I don't know when we can get out. How are you?"

I lied and told her I was fine.

"We'll get there," she said, "just as soon as we can."

Just knowing she and Brent were coming comforted me.

I showered then stood and stared into my closet. I had to wear something, but what? All color had been bleached out of the world. Everything looked dowdy and grey. I grabbed comfortable clothes and dressed. I packed a small bag as I planned to stay with Laura and the boys. Like a robot, I began to go through the motions of daily life.

Doug and John picked me up and we went to the chapel. Albert's choice was a wise one. He would have us participate in an ancient ritual. We are not that far removed from primitive man, for whom ritual was a natural part of living. We still find life and death a mystery and try to hide behind a façade of sophistication. Rituals, regardless of the belief system involved, allow us to move out of ourselves in a formalized way. The routines are familiar, thus freeing us from having to think and make decisions. I could not be trusted to do any thinking, for I was numb with grief. In ritual, the symbols and sounds create an integrated expression of body and mind. Those simple, homely things we do on a routine basis can bring solace.

In the chapel, we were a small silent group, weak with our wounds of death. Doug was the only person who had seen Bill. For the rest of us there was something macabre about it all. Perhaps in this simple service we could begin to face the truth, begin to heal that gaping hole where life had been torn away.

In the practice of a known ritual, acceptance of the unknown becomes easier. Leonard Bernstein felt we were in an age without ritual. In the writing of his musical *Mass*, he combined jazz, rock, and Broadway with the liturgical text of the mass in order to allow people to confront the issue of what faith meant to them. I had no idea at that moment what my faith was. My whole life had been wiped away when I heard the words "Bill is dead." Maybe someday I would understand. For now, I would just get through the days.

There's a widespread notion to do away with the trappings of death—viewing bodies, coffins, services, etc. Perhaps if one doesn't have to deal with those trappings the pain will be lessened. Death will lose its sting, if we could pretend he had just gone away for an extended holiday.

A friend who knew I was working on this book called to encourage me to finish. Then she told of talking with a man who sat beside her on her recent flight. He seemed depressed and she asked what was wrong. He told her he was returning from a funeral. His nephew, aged 21, had committed suicide. My friend sympathized and asked how the family was coping. "It's my sister, his mother," he said. "I'm worried about her. She won't admit it's happened. She said she's pretending he's just gone to Australia. That's what she's telling people." My friend told him about me and my book. "Give her this," he told her as he scribbled his name and phone number on a scrap of paper. "If she needs any encouragement, tell her to call."

He knew that pretending his nephew was just gone may bring temporary relief, but does not allow for healing. Those who have a dear one listed as missing in action know the horror of the unknown. The truth, when the death is known, may hit with a crushing blow, but it is a clean one from which you can recover. The unknown is like a cancer deep within, working unobserved, growing in a dangerous way. There is no health in the lie, no chance to heal from the hurt. Wounds left untended fester and turn gangrenous and the patient dies.

Denial is a natural first response. But I couldn't stay in denial too long, for that would hamper, even stop my healing process. The energy it takes to suppress the truth is energy needed to go on living. In denial, some of 'you' isn't available to anyone or any task. You have to use part of 'you' to keep the truth suppressed. I knew, deep down, that I would know what was best for us, and if I didn't have answers, I'd find them. We have wisdom within us waiting to be tapped. And we are surrounded by sources that can provide answers.

I could not, would not, pretend, nor hide my head in the sand. As painful as it would be, I would keep facing reality.

Albert, looking older and more dignified in his white robes, called us together. "Blessed be God: Father, Son, and Holy Spirit."

Numbly, I read aloud from the Prayer Book, "And blessed be His kingdom, now and forever."[4] My will and intellect were numb. I went through the motions, allowing Albert to set the pace, grateful for the words of peace. It was comforting to not have to think.

"O God of grace and glory, we remember before you this day our brother Bill. We thank you for giving him to us, his family and friends, to know and to love as a companion on our earthly pilgrimage. In your boundless compassion, console us who mourn. Give us faith to see in death the gate of eternal life, so that in quiet confidence we may continue our course on earth, until, by your call, we are reunited with those who have gone before."[5]

This first private ritual of saying words from a prayer book, listening to the priest, eating the bread and drinking wine, was a symbolic one for us. There was comfort in being together, reading words written so many centuries ago, and kneeling where countless others had knelt in their grief and joy. Our bodies and voices went through familiar motions. The idea of the mystery of life, of a power source greater than we could understand or figure out gave us a context within which we could hold what was happening to us.

The service closed with Albert's reading, "Let not your heart be troubled: ye believed in God, believe also in me. In my Father's house are many mansions: if it were not so, I would have told you. I go to prepare a place for you."[6] Perhaps Bill was doing that, I thought, working on a spiritual plane to do those things he felt he had been unable to do on earth. Was this to be the culmination of Bill's search for union with God? My heart tightened as I wondered what my role in all of that spiritual searching had been.

---

[4]   The Book of Common Prayer, p. 355

[5]   Ibid., p. 493

[6]   Holy Bible, John 14:2-4

Bill was eighteen during the Vietnam War years, a scary time. We held our breath until we learned that John's number exempted him. Doug at seventeen was too young, but Bill was the right age to be drafted. We had moved again (my twelfth move, Bill's eighth), this time to Ventura, and Bill was enrolled in a nearby college. Dick's friend, a man whose life he had saved during WWII, had given him a job in his automobile dealership. The move made it impossible to go to the Quaker silent meetings Bill and I had attended in Pasadena. However, there was a Quaker couple in Ventura, and they invited us to join them Sunday mornings for their silent meeting. Bill had decided to become a conscientious objector and his friendship with this man was a godsend. The fellow had been a conscientious objector during the Second World War and so had no illusions about what happens. Nor did I. During that war, I was attending the University of Minnesota, active in the theater there. One day, three men, a student from Harvard and two professors from Yale, showed up. They were all Quakers, pacifists, conscientious objectors interested in the theater. Rather than be jailed, they had agreed to be used in an experiment conducted by a group of doctors and scientists and were housed under the University stadium. They invited a group of us to visit and I went. In the experiment, the men were being starved and had been assured that when they reached the point just before death, they would then be restored back to health.

The eldest man accepted playing the role of King Lear in one of our productions. He was marvelous and we all watched as during rehearsals and the run of the play he got thinner and thinner. I had no illusions about what it meant to be a conscientious objector and told Bill so. I asked how far he was willing to go for his beliefs. He smiled. "All the way."

Dick had been a marine in World War II. He did not approve, but would not stand in Bill's way. I told Bill he had to do this on his own, for he would stand alone before the draft board to prove his case.

Bill spent many hours with the Quaker man and he found individuals to vouch for him. He wrote his essay and made an appointment with the Draft Board. I agreed to drive him to Pasadena for his meeting.

Pasadena had made national headlines when Dr. George F. Regas, rector of All Saints Episcopal Church, had preached a sermon against the war in Vietnam. He had nearly lost his job as a result. Pasadena was filled with "Hawks." They had little time or patience for any liberal "Doves." I was nervous. I had not seen Bill's essay, as he wanted to "handle it himself." He was always saying that—doing that. He was the most independent child!

I drove us up to the building where the meeting was to be held. "You wait in the car," he told me. I watched him walk to the door, this tall handsome nineteen-year-old boy, his youthful confidence evident in his stride. Tears filled my eyes as I thought of his facing the panel of men who would decide his fate. As unpopular as the Vietnam War was with many, conscientious objectors were even more unpopular.

I waited anxiously. Was there nothing I could do? I watched the doorway, all the while pleading with God to let my son be safe.

It didn't take long. I tried to read Bill's face as he strode toward the car. He opened the passenger door. "Well?" I asked.

He climbed in, turned to me and smiled. "It's okay. They approved my being a conscientious objector."

Bill's essay and his manner had convinced the board of his sincerity. He would serve his country by volunteering his time at a residential school for emotionally disturbed children. He did, and continued serving long past his required commitment.

Bill finally shared his essay with me. It began "I believe that all people were created equally, and so everyone has the inalienable right to, in his own way, work towards self-realization or union with God."

I felt a chill as I recalled this. Was this what Bill has been seeking, I wondered? Union with God? He also wrote "I feel that the only means that show that my beliefs are deeply held is the way I live my life and the discipline that I use in it. I have never been active in political demonstrations because I feel that I must BE my philosophy and not preach it." As I thought back on this now, I saw that Bill had been seeking union with God since he was very young.

And now the little service was over and we had to face the world. I saw John begin to cry and knew he was accepting the reality of Bill's death.

Albert hugged me. "Ruth, you're strong. You know what to do for your loved ones." I knew he was right and yet dreaded being that strong. I wanted to succumb to the grief and just die. Although awake, and alert, I felt as if I were under water. It took all my strength to remain conscious.

I knew instinctively there were certain key rites to perform, rituals that would fit our family and give us a chance to express in physical ways those emotions we were feeling. We all know, in our deepest places of knowing, what is good for us, and thus can design rituals for ourselves. We could not let Bill's passage from this life go unmarked.

The rite of the Eucharist was like a tiny light that pierced the dark of our denial. Our Bill was dead and we would have to live with that truth. Long ago I'd read about Dietrich Bonhoeffer, the Lutheran theologian executed by the Nazis. Bonhoeffer wrote that nothing ever fills the gap left by a loved one, and it would be wrong to find a substitute. We should keep it open, to simply hold out and see the grief through. That way we keep alive our communion, even at the cost of pain. I knew even then that somehow I will spend a lifetime learning to live with this.

But now Laura needed me. My children and precious grandchildren did as well. I picked up my wounded heart and like women for thousands of years before me would be strong for my family.

Chapter Eight

After the service in the Chapel, my niece Ruthi drove me to Laura's home. The freeway was crowded. *Who are all these people?* I wondered. We passed a car filled with laughing people. *How dare they laugh?* I thought. *My son is dead. How can life go on?* For me, life had stopped. I didn't want to do anything, felt emotionally dead. *Let someone else do it*, I thought. *I have been battered, beaten up, abandoned by God. I don't even want to try any more.* I had done the best I could and this was my reward! I wanted to turn my back on God and life.

But on several occasions Albert had said, "You know what to do, and you will do it." I had not wanted to hear that. I did not want to be responsible. *Let someone else take care of everything*, I thought, but there was Laura and her children, my grandchildren. And there were my other children and Bill's friends who needed me. In order to be able to respond and react spontaneously and appropriately, I needed to let my consciousness back in. From somewhere in my depths I needed to find the courage to move back into life and living. Somehow I had to draw strength and courage to take care of my family, to help heal the wounds. I knew I'd have to sink deeply into my grief, experience it all, and at the same time hold myself erect like a pillar of strength for others. Could I do it? I didn't know. I could only try. In my heart I felt that we would not just survive this tragedy, but would find ways to have life again be full and meaningful. And so I stretched myself.

The stretch is healthy, for if we behave exclusively out of our own need, we become self-indulgent and stop our healing process. If we live only to model or show an exterior, we cover the wounds so they fester from within and eventually cause damage. To try to keep up a "good show" makes a mockery of living. Both an interior and exterior expression of living is necessary. Few will manage a perfect 50-50 balance. It is enough to be aware of the dichotomy and in that awareness move from interior to exterior when appropriate.

We watched to see that everyone was maintaining a balance, allowing ourselves at first to be heavily weighted toward the private, inner grief. Gradually, we moved toward that public expression of living.

It is frightening to move back into life, to open oneself to caring and loving. But it is necessary to do so. To consciously be willing to be a role model takes courage. We learn to live by observing the models we have around us. So I needed to be willing.

We finally arrived at Laura's home and there she was, beautiful and courageous, she and her children waiting for me, needing me. Every part of me wanted to just disappear and I wondered where I'd find the energy to do what I needed to do. John and Doug were there in the background, doing whatever was needed. Bill's friends were there and their love for him was like balm. We needed each other and because of them and my family I would find the strength to be responsible. I would live, one step at a time.

I had wonderful role models to turn to, all those women in history before me who had faced grief and tragedy, and had survived with dignity. But that knowledge was of little use to me, as my heart was broken. The fragile threads of faith in God had been torn asunder. Those women in their grief would not get me through these days. It was my family's need that would. I kept thinking in clichés, those timeworn words of courage and strength I'd heard all my life. I would have to put them into action, stretch myself beyond what I thought was my breaking point.

While with the family, I noticed we all watched each other carefully to make sure we were okay. Alec, at two, loved having the house full of people. It was like a party. There were gifts for the children and loving arms that hugged and played. Alec was well occupied. Spencer, at four, had a better understanding of what was going on. He came to me and hugged me. "Dad came to me last night," he whispered in my ear.

"He did?" I said. "What did he do?"

"He said he loved me and he tickled me."

I hugged Spencer back.

He then climbed onto his mother's lap and took her face in his hands. "Don't cry," he said. "Please don't cry."

"Sometimes you just have to cry," she said and hugged him.

At one point during the day I saw that Spencer was acting strangely, as if he was uncomfortable in his own skin. He was making faces and odd contortions. "Laura," I said. "What have you told Spencer about Bill's death?"

"I told him that his dad had died and was in heaven."

"Well," I said. "He's listening to all the conversations and can't figure them out. You need to talk to him." I had learned long ago that children aren't taken in by our superficial conversations. They look beneath the words, and pick up from the ether what is really going on. You can't fool them.

Laura took Spencer into the kitchen. I stepped inside and closed the door. She kneeled before him, held his arms and said, "Spencer, Dad isn't coming back. Do you understand?"

I saw the truth hit him, saw him tremble. Then he nodded. "I understand."

"But I promise you that I will never leave you."

"Promise?"

She nodded. "Promise."

My heart ached for this little family. Children are so vulnerable, so dependent upon the adults around them for their support and love. But so are we who are adult. We never outgrow that need. As torn as I was in my grief, I gathered them in my arms and hoped my age and strength would be a haven for them.

Spencer missed his father terribly, both boys did. They had been very close. Laura would find good therapists to help the boys sort out their grief, but for now many loving arms were comforting. The school therapist eventually helped Laura talk to the children about their father's suicide, for they needed to know the truth.

A psychologist from Spencer's school had Spencer and Alec draw wild angry marks on large pieces of paper. She let them stamp their feet and show with their bodies how angry they were that their dad wasn't coming back. Spencer's piano teacher is also a musical therapist. She had Spencer compose pieces to express his feelings of sorrow, loss, and anger, safe ways to act out his deep feelings.

A snowstorm had delayed Mary and Brent's arrival. When I saw Mary, she burst into tears. "Oh, Mom, did you get the book I sent?"

"Yes."

"Oh, Mom, I never meant to hurt . . ."

"It was perfect," I said. "In reading it I was able to grieve the loss of my baby." She is a mother. She understood. We held one another silently, letting our hearts commune.

I thought about how tightly we are all connected, how in some mysterious way we know everything, and yet choose to live our lives merely connecting at a surface level. Mary told me that for several days before Bill's death, she had felt horrible and had been thinking about him. She and Bill had not been close as children. They had waged a quiet battle for my attention. At the dinner table, they sat on either side of me. John and Doug didn't seem to notice or care. Not until they were adults had Mary and Bill made up. One of my favorite pictures of them was taken at one of our family reunions. They are talking, smiling at one another. The picture was taken against the backlight of the fireplace and the glow of flames reflected warmly on their faces.

During the time around Bill's death, our whole family seemed to be operating in an extrasensory kind of way. Mary had seen that little book in a bookstore and sent it to me. I got it at exactly the time when I needed it to help me grieve. Doug had called Bill's office the day of Bill's death. He never called Bill there, always called his home. Even my mother had somehow tuned in. She had called me, something she never did.

We are more than just physical bodies. There is so much we cannot explain. Throughout my life, my dreams had given me messages. Meditation and prayer do also. And there are some practices and exercises that allow us to go very deep within our consciousness. I knew this was also true for Bill. One of the most unexpected messages from him came after he had completed Erhard's est Training. Bill had asked me, "Did I have a twin brother?"

I was stunned. I had never told him about that. There was a twin. After Bill's delivery, I had a terrible backache. My mother was caring for my children, and I could tell by the sound of her voice that she was in trouble. I needed to go home so I could relieve her. So against my doctor's wishes, I checked myself out of the hospital. Two days later, I rushed into my bathroom. It felt like my insides were coming out. There, I delivered the small dead twin. I took the fetus to the doctor and told Dick, my mother and no one else.

Now Bill was telling me that he had killed this brother.

"Oh, Bill, no," I said. "It's very common that a second baby doesn't survive. You didn't kill anyone."

But Bill shook his head. "As I was being born, I knew only one of us could make it. I kept thinking, 'I'm not going to make it, I'm not going to make it.' I killed him."

There was no talking him out of it.

My friend Patrick finally arrived and joined the others in comforting and caring for all who had gathered. It felt like angels were all over the place, taking care of all the details. Bill's boss at Imagine Films had arranged for caterers who specialized in healthy organic food to supply meals, which they did for weeks. At one point, our friend Patty said she had always heard that God was love. Now, she was seeing that love in action.

Doug's maturity amazed me. He kept taking care of us. He's the one who identified Bill, who arranged and paid for the cremation. His steely strength manifested his compassion for us all. At Laura's, he took me aside and told me what he knew about the suicide.

Apparently, Bill had driven to his office that early morning of March 2nd, and typed two letters and the Rilke poem. One of the letters was left on his boss Terry's desk. Then he went to the YMCA, swam, had a sauna, and meditated. He left and made arrangements to have his briefcase containing a letter, a poem, his wallet, appointment book, and glasses delivered. His instructions were specific. The briefcase was to be filled with white roses and freesias, and delivered to Laura that afternoon at 2:00 while the children were in nursery school. The messenger service had no questions, for they had made numerous deliveries for Bill.

What he did the rest of that day we do not know for sure. My guess is that he drove to a lonely lookout spot to meditate and say good-bye, for he was a conscientious, spiritual man. By 2:00 that afternoon he was in the bank parking lot, his car facing the hospital window where the two sons he so loved had been born. He placed the car papers on the seat to be readily available for the authorities, took hold of the steering wheel, and as Laura read his letter, drank a large dose of strychnine mixed with organic fruit juice.

On Saturday afternoon, after Mary and Brent's arrival, Doug gathered us together in Laura's bedroom. We all sat on the big bed, holding hands to be close. Laura told us what had happened the night before Bill's death. She said he had been quiet and pale for some time. On Wednesday night, she told him she was afraid he was having an affair, was going to kill himself, or had embezzled money. She said he laughed and said he was not having an affair, and had not embezzled money. He didn't say anything about suicide, but that was so outside the possibilities of anything she thought he'd ever do, she said nothing. Bill said he had to work it out by himself. Laura told us she was worried because he'd been sick with bronchitis since Christmas, and yet never missed a day of work or any time with the children. She had a strong sense that evening she should just let him be. But, she said, the look on his face was one of desolation.

Then Laura showed us Bill's letter. It was in a dark grey presentation folder, the typed words stark against the white bond paper. "Dearest <u>Laura</u>, <u>Spencer</u>, <u>and Alec</u>," it began. "I am aware of the implicit privilege it has been to live with you. Each of you is an incredible person. You deserve more than I am able to provide. You are each whole and complete and I love you. It is time for me to go back to the infinite void. Love, Max [Laura's nickname for Bill]." He had added a postscript, apologizing for the terrible shock. ". . . it is my wish that it be as easy and acceptable as possible (so what else is new). As you know, I wish a quick and quiet cremation with as little outcry as possible." In the left pocket of the folder was the poem by Rainer Maria Rilke:

> "Be patient toward all that is unsolved in your heart
> And try to love the questions themselves.
> Do not now seek the answers that cannot be given you
> Because you would not be able to live them.
> And the point is to live everything.
> Live the questions now.
> Perhaps you will gradually,
> Without noticing it,
> Live along some distant day
> Into the answer."

Leaving the poem was so like Bill. He knew we'd need it. We waited as each person read the letter. When we were finished, Laura lovingly placed it back into the folder. "When the boys are older, they'll want to see it," she said. "I'll save it for them."

"Have you seen him?" my daughter asked. Mary and Brent, in their young lives, were far more familiar with death than I. Brent's mother had died after a long battle with cancer. His brother had died suddenly, leaving a wife pregnant with their fifth child. Mary had comforted her husband and his family through their ordeals of grief. Then she had nursed Brent's sister Kris, her dearest friend, the only sister Mary ever had, through her terminal illness. She had been with her when she died at age 32 of breast cancer, and had awakened the three little girls, aged seven, five, and two, to say goodbye to their mother. The specter of death had haunted my daughter in a way I could only wonder about.

"You should see him, Mom," she said through her tears, and she hugged me.

I dreaded seeing Bill's body. I had been warned that people who died from poison were hideously distorted. I wanted to remember him tall and handsome, alive. But in a primal way I knew we needed to see him.

Doug kneeled beside Laura and took her hands. "Do you want to see him?"

She pulled away. "No."

Gently, Doug again took Laura's hands. "You might want to say goodbye."

She looked at me, her dark eyes bright with tears. "What do you think?"

"We need to see him," I said.

"We need to say goodbye," John said and choked over his tears.

Laura turned to Doug. "I don't want them to pretty him up. I want to see him just the way he is." Doug promised they would not touch him.

That goodbye was necessary for us who were living as well as for our dear one. We needed to not only let him go, but to encourage him to go to the Light. Just as the umbilical cord had been cut at birth in order for Bill to live, this "silver" cord of life had to be cut so we could truly live, and Bill could go on to wherever he needed to go. As difficult as it would be, we needed to see Bill. Any sparks of denial needed to be put out so we who were left behind could go on living.

Doug, John, and Brent made arrangements at the funeral home. Doug drove me, holding my hand all the way. They went in first to make sure everything was all right. Then we followed.

Bill was on a gurney, covered with a pale blue cloth that came to the floor. Two indirect lamps shed a pale light, one at his head, the other at his feet. Doug went up and uncovered his face. John gasped. "He's home. I don't think he was ever at home here."

Bill's hair fell in long golden brown waves. His arms were crossed over his chest, his long toes pointing up beneath the blue cloth, like the stone effigies of kings and knights I'd seen in the cathedrals of England. Handsome in life, he was regal in death.

We let Laura go up to be with him. Then it was my turn. I hugged and kissed him and sobbed. Then a sense of peace came over me, and I really looked at him. It took my breath away. He looked like a king with a maturity and grace I'd never seen before. He was so at peace, so beautiful. His eyes were closed, his face at rest. I stared, wanting to imprint his features forever in my mind, to never forget his dark brown eyes, the impish smile he was always trying to hide. I kissed him again, and promised that his memory would never diminish in any way. Then his brothers and sister went forward to be with him, humbled in the face of death.

Those final moments have a potency to them, marking our hearts forever. We are helpless in the face of death, for it reflects to us the mystery of life.

We sat in the room and a peaceful silence descended on us all. Laura looked at me and smiled. "He'll soon be running things up there."

We laughed.

"Yes," Doug said. "He probably just took in a new organizational plan to the boss."

Bill had actually done that at Imagine Films shortly after he was hired. They'd not only implemented the plan, but had given Bill and his boss substantial raises in pay.

"Remember Bill's eighth birthday?" I said. "John, Mary, and Doug surprised us all with an alligator in a large bowl."

John laughed as he remembered. "We knew you wouldn't do it," he said.

"Well, you're right about that," I said. "Bill named it Checkie because its underside was checkered. It had to be force-fed and Bill made me help. He'd open its jaws and I'd stuff pieces of fresh fish down its gullet with a toothpick. I was scared to death of it, and your dad wouldn't even go near it." I smiled remembering. "Bill insisted I buy fresh fish which he then cut up into tiny pieces and froze in aluminum foil. We had enough frozen fish for a zoo. At night when I'd go in to check Bill, that little creature would raise its head and hiss at me. I actually grew to admire it. Brave little thing. But it died, and Bill and I cried together over it. He buried it in the backyard in the little cemetery under the rose bush."

We sat quietly together. "Well, he's not coming back," Laura said, and reminded us of the ceremony Bill had produced for His Holiness The 16th Gyalwa Karmapa, a leader of one of Tibetan Buddhism's four major schools of spiritual teachings, the Kagyu lineage. Werner Erhard had arranged for the Karmapa to come from Tibet to Los Angeles to perform, along with his monks, the Black Crown Ceremony. The Karmapa has a role similar to that of the Dalai Lama in that he is the spiritual leader of a specific Buddhist sect. Karmapa means "the embodiment of all the activities of the buddhas."[7]

---

[7]   http://www.kagyuoffice.org/kagyulineage.karmapa16.html

The Black Crown, also known as the Vajra Crown, is an attribute of the Karmapas, which signifies the power to help all beings. They claim that the female Buddhas bestowed this energy field on Karmapa at his enlightenment several thousand years ago. The replica shown at ceremonies has the power to open the subconscious of those present and permits the Karmapa to exchange his limitless space-awareness for beings' inhibitions and pain. It is a means for gaining liberation through seeing.

A well-known actor gave the Karmapa the use of his home in Los Angeles, and I joined a number of assistants who helped. I spent several days making the butter tea the monks loved and cooking pan after pan of bacon. In the afternoons we were invited to meditations on the spacious lawn behind the house.

The ceremony of the Black Crown was held in the Pasadena Convention Center, which holds 3,000 people. It was packed, standing room only. Everything worked flawlessly. Laura said that, at the completion of the ceremony, the Karmapa told Bill he was off the wheel as he had produced a perfect event. Doing so, Bill had completed his missions in life. He would not need to return.

As I sat in the quiet of that room with Bill and his family, sentences from his essay, the one he'd written for the draft board, came to mind. ". . . I acquired the belief that if I would just have faith, that God would reveal himself to me." Had he lost that faith? What had God revealed? "The Quaker way is so to order the inner life so that there will be a proper balance of inner and outer life, inner holding first place." Had he fallen out of balance? "I feel that I must BE my philosophy and not preach it." Was that why he was so quiet about himself? "I try to live my life the way I think God would have me live it . . ." Was he seeking to be perfect?

My heart cried out to this son who had worked so hard to be what he thought God would have him be. I had followed a similar spiritual path, but I had not gone this far. What had happened? Had he indeed gone home? Why had he killed himself? Why?

Chapter Nine

Laura, John, Doug, and I went through Bill's things, deciding who wanted what. Laura insisted that John and Doug take some of the clothes, as she did not want anything wasted. "I'm saving his leather jacket," she said. "Maybe one of the boys will want it someday."

We each took things we wanted. It was a way of having a part of Bill with us. I have something of his in every room in my house. It comforts me when I see these items.

Patrick, Albert, and I began to plan a funeral service for Bill. We included those passages we felt appropriate. The prayer of St. Francis of Assisi had been one of Bill's favorites. We wrote it in. In all things I consulted with Laura. We had always been friends, but now a bond existed that nothing would ever damage.

On Sunday morning, I was seated at my desk, while Patrick worked at the computer. Albert had stepped out of the room to get another cup of tea. I glanced at the digital clock. It had been a gift to my husband from Henry Mancini and I liked its simplicity. As the numbers dropped to read 2:00 I felt a murmur go through me. "*He's free,*" I whispered. Then I realized it had been exactly three days on the hour since his death. When I shared my realization with Patrick he told me he'd heard that the soul lingered for three days before moving on. I was sure that had happened. Bill had moved on into realms I could only imagine.

Many families can allow the established institutions and organizations they are part of to handle all of the details at the time of a death—church, funeral parlor, etc. Our death was a suicide and the police were involved. I knew my church would not make any distinctions regarding that, nor would the funeral parlor. But my family's backgrounds and experiences were so diverse, so rich, that no one institution or establishment could speak for all of us. We would create our own rituals.

We needed to mourn our loss, to say goodbye, to be assured our loved one was taken care of. We also needed to allow others to grieve and show their love and respect in manners meaningful for them as well as for us.

In the immediate family were religious views from agnostic through mainline Christian, as well as Jewish and Roman Catholic. Bill's friends were diverse: Quakers, several kinds of Buddhists, atheists, devout Christians, Jews, agnostics, and New Age. Many were the voices that would bid him on his way.

Our funeral plans followed the Episcopal rites. Rituals allow you to take the thoughts and images racing around in your head and manifest them in a physical manner in the world—your world. Even to participate in an unfamiliar rite is centering. We chose those rites that spoke to our history and culture.

The funeral allowed us to mourn our loss, to commend the soul of our loved one to God, and to return to living. The musical requiems that have been written begin, *Requiem aeternam dona eis, Domine, et lux perpetua luceat eis.* "Oh, God. Grant them eternal rest in peace and light eternal shine upon them." The music and words then dramatically implore God to protect the soul from the torments of hell, and to remember the promise of resurrection. I did not want my son having to face the torments of hell. Not that sweet peaceful man!

I prefer the form of Herbert Howells' *Hymnus Paradisi* which he wrote in memory of his only son who died when just nine years old. Howells' libretto ignores hell entirely. The score seems more the plea of a parent for strength to go on living and trusting, and the request that his dead son now rest forever in the Light. That was my request.

The words of the funeral service assured me that Bill's soul was commended to God. In my heart I cried out, "Oh, God, don't hurt him."

Patrick had to return to Phoenix, but not until he had copies made of the service for the funeral. He printed out the liturgy that Laura and I chose, along with one of Bill's last pieces of artwork. When I had first seen Bill's art works, I had thought they were intriguing. Now, after his death, I saw them as prescient. The one Patrick chose was a drawing of Bill in his tuxedo. There are four images on the page, each one fainter and less distinct, with the last falling off the paper. When John saw it, he said that Bill was trying to tell us something. Now we saw it. Too late.

That Sunday evening, the family and Bill's best friends Sandy and Donna gathered in the choir stalls of All Saints Church in Pasadena. It was more intimate. There had been a wedding the day before, and the church was filled with white flowers. My friends Marta, Arthur, and Nancy had brought dozens of white roses and placed them on top of the ebony grand piano. The Chinese use white at a death rather than black. I also felt strongly that Bill was now graduating into something beyond our understanding. White seemed to be appropriate. In my need to have some sanity in my life again, I grasped at everything as healing, communicating something, or being a lesson for me, anything that could help put my life back into some sort of balance.

It is natural for healing to take place, for scars to blend in again with the landscape, and ugly edges to soften with weathering. We had been left with an ugly wound, and we needed to let everything in the universe begin a healing process. We needed to restore sanity to our lives. In my weakness, I merely surrendered to that which was greater than I, a Higher Power, a force I didn't fully understand.

My friend Clarke Oler, one of the priests at All Saints, asked to help officiate, and added a stately presence. Again, Albert was wonderful, and his homily was appropriate and comforting. He read two scriptures. These referred to the traditions about the founding of the Christian Church. The most familiar was the story that Jesus said to Peter, "Upon this rock I will build my church."

The other tradition comes from the description of Jesus on the cross. It is said that when he was dying he called out to his mother and best friend, "Mother, behold your son. Son, behold your mother." The two left and formed a new community out of which grew the early church.

We were a new community. We turned to one another to give and to receive, knowing we all were growing in our wisdom and experience. In the ritual of the funeral we showed our community and shared together our grief. As a family, we commended Bill to God, to Light perpetual.

Sandy played *Rainbows*, a song he had written for Bill and Laura's wedding. Donna read Rilke's poem about living with the question.

Clarke read the words: "Into your hands, O merciful Savior, we commend your servant Bill. Acknowledge, we humbly beseech you, a sheep of your own fold, a lamb of your own flock, a sinner of your own redeeming. Receive him into the arms of your mercy, into the blessed rest of everlasting peace, and into the glorious company of the saints in light. Amen. May his soul and the souls of all the departed, through the mercy of God, rest in peace. Amen."[8]

I felt like a parent who had been called into the principal's office. I was willing to admit my son had done something wrong, but I also felt like I must protect him from unjust treatment. I was pleased to hear the words said aloud that he could rest in the Light in peace.

Now we had to take care of the living. I chose a song Bill had liked, written by Clarke's son Kim. The words had been inspired by astronaut Russell Schweikert on his return from orbit on a NASA space flight. As Bill had returned to his spiritual home, we would return to our earthly one.

> *For the earth forever turning,*
> *For the land, for skies and sea;*
> *To our Lord we sing returning home*
> *To our blue green hills of earth.*
> *For the mountains, hills and pastures*
> *In their silent majesty;*
> *For the stars, for all the heavens*
> *Sing we our joyful praise to Thee.*
> *For sun, for rain and thunder,*
> *For the season's harmony;*
> *For our lives, for all creation*
> *Sing we our joyful praise to Thee.*
> *For the earth forever turning,*
> *For the land which gave us birth,*
> *To our Lord we sing returning*
> *Home to the blue green hills of earth.*[9]

We closed with Psalm 150, a Psalm to life. It was necessary to remind us again of this mystery. That rather than have life or death, we had a context within which we could hold both, for life *is* living *and* dying. We made our public farewell, confirmed that it was "goodbye."

I held Laura's hand throughout the service. At the end, she squeezed my hand and said, "This is what has been missing. I feel complete now."

---

[8]   The Book of Common Prayer, p. 465

[9]   Paul Winter Consort, *Missa Gaia* (Earth Mass)

After the service we did what families do. We went to my home for a meal and a chance to talk about Bill. My sister Mary Ann, her daughter Ruthi, and daughter-in-law Denny brought food for a good old-fashioned wake. Bill's father, with his current wife, was there. The shock of Bill's death had unnerved him. He seemed suddenly old and feeble. As families through the ages have done, we told our anecdotes and stories, laughing and crying together, our first real task of living.

The finality of the funeral opened a way for me to begin to release the stress of the impact of Bill's death. That night, after everyone had gone, a friend held me as I trembled and shook. Tears coursed down my cheeks and every muscle seemed to dance as it let go of the tension. I knew I was reacting to the impact my body had received on hearing the news of Bill's death. That kind of news has an impact on our bodies as hard as being run through with a sword. We react to that with muscles tensing, the mind shutting out awareness. But our neurological systems record it all and store it until it is safe again to let us become aware. Some soldiers experience this kind of reaction months after returning from combat. Some incidents are never exhumed and may lie dormant within us, never causing a problem. But strong feelings need to be experienced in order to complete and leave us free to continue living.

Chapter Ten

Now Bill's friends also needed a chance to say goodbye and so they planned a Memorial Service. Spencer, Bill's four-year-old son, chose the music. Despite his young age, he knew what his dad liked best—the Roaches, Talking Heads, Vivaldi, Bach, and Sandy's compositions. They had shared their love of music. Sandy, Spencer's godfather, and a jazz musician, helped Spencer make a tape to use at the Memorial. Spencer kept the tape for himself, a way to continue to share with his dad whom he missed terribly. Involving the children helped them better understand what was going on. Although they hadn't attended the formal funeral, they came to the Memorial. Two-year-old Alec thought it was another big party, but Spencer seemed to realize that all of these people had come to remember his dad, and he was pleased.

Spencer and Alec live now with suicide as an option, a fact few children must face. We have realized the need to be open in our communication with them and with one another. Secrets can have a deadly consequence.

Writer and minister Frederick Buechner tells of how one morning his father put on gray slacks and a blue sweater, stuck his head in Frederick's bedroom door and said goodbye. Then he went to the garage and calmly asphyxiated himself. There was no funeral, no talk of his death. In her grief and shock, his mother took her sons to live in Bermuda, as far away from the tragic scene as she could go. His father's pictures were destroyed. Only as an adult did Buechner learn how his father had died. The death, the suicide, as tragic as it was, was not the difficulty. It was the secrecy. His father had just disappeared from their lives and their conversations. He was never mentioned again. We would not make that mistake. At the same time, we would not dwell on the suicide nor be morbid about it.

The large room where the Memorial was held was packed. Laura laughed. "It's a good thing Max was cremated so he can't roll over in his grave." He would not have felt comfortable with all of the attention. Doug led the Memorial, and began by reminding everyone that Bill had taken his own life, and only in honesty could we maintain the healing that was taking place. He suggested that this would be an opportunity for people to complete their relationship with Bill. People were encouraged to share whatever they wanted, and they did.

I had feared it would be hard to hold up my head, with no excuses or justifications, and not be shamed by the suicide. Our culture still holds that act as a shameful one. I need not have worried. What became very evident was that my son was loved. Many of the people said they had not gotten very close to him personally, he was such a private person, but they admired and respected him. They honored his integrity, style, gentle compassion, and loving manner. Apparently he was available to everyone, was ethical and clean in his relationships. It sounded to me like he'd taken care of everyone except himself.

I was deeply moved by the stories. They were funny, poignant, and touching. Bill had not only been expert at what he did, he had been generous, spiritual, thoughtful, and funny—sometimes zany. We all cried and laughed together, our tears and joy salving the wounds we had, for death touches us all. John Donne, in his Meditation xvii, wrote it perfectly—ask not for whom the bell tolls for it tolls for thee.

Bill's friend Buzz stood. "I'll never forget Bill," he said. "We once had to fix a thermostat for a seminar room. Now, I've got a Ph.D. in nuclear physics, and when Bill told me what we had to do I told him there was no way it could be done. I was positive it couldn't be done." Buzz laughed. "Next thing I knew, he had fixed it."

That was so like Bill, I thought. "I'll take care of it," was what he had always said. Had his suicide been his way of doing that, taking care of whatever had made his look one of desolation? Some time after Bill's death, a detective called Doug and said they'd discovered where Bill had bought the poison. He had signed for it, used his own name. When I heard the date I was stunned. Bill had bought the poison in November. He killed himself in March. Had we but known of his struggles with depression could we have helped? Even today, my eyes fill with tears when I think of that. How could we have helped? Would he even have let us try?

At the Memorial, Donna told of a time when she, Sandy, and Bill had been out together and ended up at Sandy's house. As they entered the kitchen, Bill tapped out a rhythm on the toaster with one hand, and then with the other beat a tempo on the refrigerator. Sandy picked up the beat on the stove, and Donna joined them on the cupboard. Donna laughed remembering. They "played" nearly every item in the house, ending up laughing hysterically.

"He wasn't much for talking," Sandy said. "As close as we were, I think I was his best friend, he never revealed much of himself to me. But actions speak louder than words, and he displayed his friendship in the many things he did. I felt privileged to be his friend and godfather to his sons."

Laura, standing at the side with Alec, spoke. "Doug and I were talking last night about Bill. I know how hard this is for all of you, but I want you to know that Bill is fine. One of the things he loved to do was to go to the Samadhi Isolation tanks. You know, those tanks where you float in tepid water and it's pitch black. It's where you can't tell where you end and the universe begins. I did it once and said never again. But Bill liked it. He could completely relax and be at one with the universe. I think he's always wanted to be at one with God. Well, he just bought himself the biggest tank available. I think he's finally at one with the universe."

One needs to hear the comments and stories shared by friends and contemporaries in order to know the complete person. The stories did that and allowed me to have a fuller sense of my son.

Bill's dream job had come through when he had been hired by Imagine Films. The company was marvelous. They catered the Memorial along with sending food to Laura's home. Bill's boss set up a memorial fund for the boys, to which they contributed generously. In a business not known for its thoughtfulness, they were more than kind to Bill's memory. He had been respected and appreciated by his employers, and they would miss him. In his letter to Laura, the Vice President of Marketing wrote, "Dear Laura, Alec, and Spencer, I wanted to write you a note telling you how Bill impacted my life in the past six months that we knew each other. Available, accessible, totally organized and always sensitive to everyone's needs from early morning until late at night. Bill was on his way to being the very best at what is expected of his profession, and he became a major source of answers to production problems. I know I will miss him very much, but I know I will remember him for the class, style and integrity that he brought to work—every day."

The Senior Vice President wrote of Bill's high standards of professionalism. But he also wrote, "More importantly, on a personal level I found Bill to be a kind, generous and helpful person . . ."

The first letter I received came from my dear friend Judy. "How he must have suffered!" she wrote. The words jarred me, and I dropped the note. A feeling of guilt washed over me. Why hadn't I known? I stared at the note and thought about Judy. She must have known first-hand about that kind of suffering for she had those days when she locked herself away in a darkened room. My heart now ached also for her. Bill's first serious girlfriend wrote a beautiful letter about him and recommended that I read the book *Solitude: A Return to the Self* by Anthony Storr. "He was so quiet," she wrote, "and so kind."

I clutched these letters, and the scraps of humor and love spoken about Bill, as to a life support system. We needed these demonstrations to be able to continue on in our lives. No matter whether eloquent, or simple and plain, they were like a life force for us, reminding us again of this man we had loved and cherished.

Laura found some papers Bill had written before his death. "I think it's a draft of a suicide note," she told me. The draft read, "My apologies for this impersonal good bye. Please give my same regrets and apology to Terry [Bill's boss] when you speak. I left a note for him for his eyes only on my desk. This is a new beginning . . . It is all possible . . . more than ever before. You will miss me but please let it go . . . it is all before you. This is an ancient spirit on a dying planet."

She also gave me a slip of paper, a note she had written. "Said in his sleep by Max on 10/15/85 at 6 am. 'If you hear a strange noise—gather two more just like it. They're giving a tour of the universe and it begins with what's in your hands.'"

Juan Pablo Mobili had known Bill and Laura when they lived in Manhattan. Juan sent a poem:

> *stones*
> *for ruth & bill maxwell*
> *the mother knows*
> *a son*
> *is her most tender limb*
>
> *silence is*
> *emptier*
> *without him*

there is no outside
to grief

no end to stones.

There was truly no outside to my grief.

We had taken care of Bill's soul and his memory with friends and family.
Now we needed to take care of his body, his mortal remains.

Chapter Eleven

We had lived all over this country, modern corporate gypsies, calling where we "hung our hats" home. So we had to find a place to bury Bill's ashes. I wanted to know where his remains were buried, for it would be a comfort for me to think of the place. Bill didn't care. He had at last made union with the Absolute, but we were still locked in a time-space dimension and needed to honor that. And so on his birth date, ten days after his death, we chose a place for his burial. Another opportunity to create a ritual for our healing.

Doug is a climber, backpacker, who had been roaming the mountains of the West since his teens. He would be the person who would know best, and so he chose the vicinity. We prepared a picnic lunch and drove to the appointed site.

We parked the cars and then Doug and Spencer led the way. Although my state was still one of shock and grief, I noticed that spring had arrived. Tiny flowers were appearing, and the birds seemed joyous in their song.

We arrived at a small grassy opening in the mountains, ringed by trees. Doug and Spencer looked the area over carefully. "What do you think?" Doug asked.

"I think this is the place," Spencer replied confidently.

At the far end was a large evergreen, its boughs forming a shaded area. Doug found a spot beneath a low branch where the ground was soft. "We'll bury him here," he said.

I had brought my gardening trowels. This was my son. I wanted to be as involved as possible in all that happened to him. Intellectually I knew that Bill had gone on, and that what was left was only the remains of the shell he'd used in this lifetime, but my heart still wanted that shell treated with respect and care.

Spencer did most of the digging, but he had each of us take a turn. Two-year-old Alec was very serious while he worked. John's daughter Chelsea, who was not yet two, did her share. She would dig a while and then toss dirt back into the hole. "No," Spencer protested. "Keep the dirt out. This is for my dad."

Finally the hole was the right size. We all stood in a circle around the grave and Doug brought out the box of ashes from his backpack. "I was about ten feet away from the mortuary," he said, "when I realized this was my brother, and I stopped and felt the weight of him," he said. He handed the box to Laura who felt the weight. She then handed it to me. It was heavier than I expected. I gave it to John, and then it went from person to person around the circle, even to the littlest children, until we all had "felt the weight" of this man.

Doug then opened the box and we all looked in. I thought the ashes would look like those from the fireplace. They didn't. They were like fine gravel, and so colorful. There were glints of turquoise, ebony, and rose among the gray. The body these had once formed had been my son, of my body, bone of my bone, blood of my blood. And now they would return to the elements they once had been. Even in this, the beauty of the universe was present.

We placed the ashes in the grave, each of us taking a handful in our turn. Spencer did most of the work. "These are my dad's ashes," he said, "and I want him buried good."

When we had finished, John brought out a large envelope. One by one he pulled out items and handed them to Spencer and Alec to place in the grave. Paper and pens for sketching, an old precious piece of wood, a lump of coal from the River Thames, sunglasses because the Light where Bill was is brilliant beyond what we can imagine, and we wanted him to always go toward the Light. There was a bit of turquoise, a piece of jade, a square of ivory, a page from the book *Be Here Now* that Bill had loved, a small silver crucifix, a bit of mirror, a Buddha, beads of every color, a blank audio tape ("So Dad can record his thoughts," Spencer said), a smooth black stone called an Apache Tear, a crystal star, ebony, money ("For treats," Alec said), candles, and a packet of matches.

Laura laughed. "Bill would have loved this. We've included all the myths. Bill was very into myths."

We stood in silence and again that sense of great peace descended on us. We placed flowers on the ground and planted some, knowing they wouldn't survive the California summer. Then John's wife said, "In my tradition (Jewish) we bring a stone." We went looking for stones. John and Doug found large ones, the rest of us smaller ones, and the little ones brought pebbles. We placed them on the ground and built a cairn.

My friend Albert says that in Ireland cairns are common. One comes across them often. "I went this way," they seem to say. "It's safe here." Markers for us who were left behind.

Again we stood in silence around the grave until that sense of calm and peace was present. And then Spencer spoke. "Now can I have a cookie?"

We laughed. Life had intruded, calling us to get back to living. We had our picnic. Sandy had brought his guitar and we sang together, celebrating living in the midst of dying, for as Rilke wrote, the "point is to live everything."

When my children were small, I could go to bed at night knowing they were all safe in bed, where they were supposed to be. I know Bill is safe and is where he's supposed to be. The place Doug chose has a clear landmark one can see for miles. He wanted me to be able to look up and see where Bill's remains are. I'm clear that at any time, in any place I can know where Bill is, but the loving gesture of my son Doug and the physical site are a comfort to me, for I still live in a world of manifested things.

Several weeks after Bill's death, I was driving my car and looked up at the mountain where he is buried. I spoke out loud. "Bill, you really gave me a challenge. I get to be the mother of a son who killed himself."

In my mind I heard him laugh. "You're up for it," he seemed to say.

I was caught up short. Was I? Was I willing to tell the truth about him and his death and still hold my head high and live? Out of the relationship I'd had with Bill, I'd better be. He had confronted me in life to be as wonderful as I was able to be. I would allow him in death to do the same. Yes, I am up for it. My grief has eased as I reach out to others in friendship and love. I draw on the strength and energy of a source greater than myself, on the ultimate power of the universe, on the mysteries that surround us. I live my life doing the best I can, forgiving myself when I fall short, and being "up for it." At the same time, I cry as I write these words, for the pain of his loss is still fresh.

I left that mountaintop with a strong sense of Bill's presence, a joyous spirit guarding and helping me.

We buried Bill on the 12th. It would have been his 36th birthday. My birthday fell on the 18th. Cynthia and Laurie, dear friends, had a party for me, with Laura and a few others. It was a video party. They showed clips from favorite movies of romances, weddings, babies, and ended with a scene from "On Golden Pond." It was a clear representation of my life, a loving reminder to continue living with the question. One late afternoon one of my graduate students stopped me in the bank parking lot. She told me how sorry she was to hear of my son's death. Then she clutched my arm. "The only way to hold this is metaphysical."

I frowned. "What?"

She sighed. "I'm a devout Catholic, married to a fine man, and have three beautiful children. I also have a good priest and an outstanding therapist, but it takes all the strength I have to keep myself on this planet. I have tried to kill myself three times and thanks be to God I have not succeeded. It's metaphysical. That's all I can say."

I told Doug about the encounter with my student. Then he told me that when Bill was eight he said he wanted to kill himself, but didn't know how. I was stunned and said, "Why didn't you tell me?"

"Mom, I was seven years old. What do you do with that kind of information when you're seven?"

I wondered if Bill had been having an internal conversation about killing himself all these years. Was that why he experimented with drugs when he was younger? Why he pursued spiritual activities? Is this what his art was expressing?

A year after Bill's death we decided to celebrate his birthday by visiting his cairn/gravesite. We packed a picnic lunch and Laura, the children, Sandy, and Donna took one car. Doug picked me up in his car and we headed up the mountain.

By March, in California, the pear trees have almost finished blooming, the cymbidium orchids are opening, and the temperature is beginning to creep up toward the 80s. I was looking forward to the drive and the chance to pay our respects to Bill. I'd brought some stones from England and friends had given me lovely rocks to place on the cairn. Suddenly we were driving through a light rain, totally unexpected. As we climbed, the rain turned to snow, and then to a blizzard. Doug stopped the car and signaled for Sandy to do likewise.

"Got chains?" Doug asked Sandy. No one did. "The Rangers will just turn us back," Doug said.

Spencer and Alec had never seen falling snow, so we all piled out and made tiny snowmen and had snowball fights. When we were thoroughly soaked, we climbed into the cars and drove to my house for a picnic.

On the ride down the mountain, I said to Doug, "Isn't that just like Bill? No memorials."

Doug laughed. "Back to life," he said.

Yes, back to life, to the request in Bill's letter to "live everything." That has been our watchword in all of this, for as much as we love and revere the dead, we are the living. We go to visit the cairn on Bill's birthday, adding stones each time, enjoying the peace there. And always we return to our daily lives, living the question.

Chapter Twelve

Laura was devastated by Bill's death. She'd had other boyfriends, some rather serious, but Bill had been the love of her life. She was strong and holding up very well, but she was lonely, and concerned, wondering about her "man karma." Her father was hospitalized with advanced Alzheimer's disease, her only brother had died tragically, and now her husband was dead. It was enough to make anyone wonder.

Laura did as I did. She grieved. We grieved together as a family, allowing our feelings to be, not needing to suppress them. And we talked often about our feelings and about Bill. But Laura was also wise. "If you go by feelings," she said, "my life is ruined—it's over." Laura knew that she could have those feelings. At the same time she made a conscious, deliberate commitment to survive this for herself and her sons, the declaration that they would grow and live fully. Then she began to live that declaration.

In June, three months after Bill's death, Laura had a birthday. I had a small gathering of women to celebrate. Laura told us that, although she is a pragmatic individual, the morning of her birthday she said aloud to Bill that she needed a gift from him, a sign to show that he knew she loved him. It was important to her, for although she'd handled her guilt regarding his suicide, it was a small nagging question that needed to be resolved.

All day she had looked and waited for some sign—anything. But nothing happened. Finally, late that evening, she went to bed weighted down with a burden of sadness. As she lay there, she noticed that the light from outside was shining on the picture of Bill on her dresser. As she looked at it, she heard Bill speak inside of her head. It was exactly the way he talked. He said she needed to take off her wedding band—that life was to go on. Laura started to cry. She said she couldn't take off her wedding ring for she had made a vow to be married to him forever. But his voice continued. He knew she loved him as he loved her, but she was to get on with her life and marry again.

I was surprised as Laura told us this, for it is not like her to dwell on spiritual matters. She held out her left hand and began to cry. It was bare.

I felt a tug in my heart. It felt like I was losing more of my son. But it was so like Bill, as if he recognized the need for us to release him better than we did ourselves. We needed to let him go on in spirit.

Just as little children have trouble understanding when mom and dad go out and leave them with a babysitter, I was having trouble understanding this realm of spirit. But understanding or not, we needed to free Bill, and we needed to free ourselves in order for life to go on in both the worldly and spiritual orders. Just as I had watched him walk away from me, first to go to school, then to go out into the world, now I had to again let him go.

Sandy had been Bill's best friend, and the suicide had been a terrible shock. In his grief, Sandy went to Laura and the boys, his godchildren, and gave them the love and friendship he'd shared with Bill.

About a year and a half after Bill's death Laura said, "Ruth, I think Sandy's falling in love with me."

I wasn't surprised. She is a beautiful woman. As Laura and Sandy grieved the loss of their dear one, the tragedy they faced together strengthened their friendship in such a way that love blossomed.

A year after that, Sandy called one Sunday morning. "Are you at home?"

I said I was.

"We'd like to come by and visit," and they did. Sandy sat on the couch beside me and took my hand. "I've come to ask for Laura's hand in marriage."

Tears filled my eyes. I was deeply moved by their thoughtfulness. "I've lost a son," I said. "It's only fair I get another."

Tears came to Sandy's eyes as he embraced me. I thought my heart might break. More of my son was fading away. *It's not fair*, I said to God. And when there was no answer, I knew that once again I had to release Bill.

Several weeks before the wedding, Spencer's teacher called Laura. "You'd better talk to Spencer (now six and a half)," she said. "Something's bothering him."

Laura sat down with Spencer. "Is there anything you want to ask me or say?"

"Actually," he said (Bill always said that), "I do. Do you think Dad knows what's going on?"

Laura hugged him. "Always, in my imagination, I see that your dad sees everything and he approves. He wants us all to be happy."

Spencer's eyes filled with tears. "I love Sandy," he said, "but I love my original dad the most."

"You must tell Sandy," Laura said.

That evening Spencer did. Sandy hugged him. "I love your original dad the most too," Sandy said, and they wept together, mourning the loss of father and dear friend. When the truth can be told and not judged or evaluated, love follows, for it flourishes in the light. Love can't be multiplied and given away, and it cannot be compared. The love Laura and her sons feel for Bill has not been a threat to the love they feel for Sandy. Rather, it has added to the bond of love they all experience. Their home has a wonderful normalcy about it; they have their ups and downs and life is going on in a daily way. The climate of love and respect there is deep and abiding. It has been tempered in the fires of death and grief. Matters of ego or control and dominance are never an issue. Sandy's "bigness" in allowing Laura and the children to love Bill has endeared him to all of us. He has truly become a son for me.

Albert, who had officiated at Bill's funeral, married Laura and Sandy. Donna, who many years previously had been Sandy's first wife and was still a best friend, stood up for him as his "best person." It was a real family affair. At the reception following the wedding, Sandy's mother came to me. "May I share those beautiful grandsons with you?" she asked. My heart swelled at the loving gesture. "Children never get enough grandmothers," I said, and I handed them over. The love those children have for me has never diminished. Love cannot be divided. It was as Albert said in the funeral homily, out of this death would come new community.

Chapter Thirteen

At the time of my son's death, my attitude about suicide reflected the attitude of society. The very air I breathed was permeated with a view that cast suicide in a moralistic, superstitious light. This attitude justifies the belief that the people who are suicidal are not like you and me. Those people must have done something wrong. Perhaps they dabbled in something forbidden or evil, or took a wrong turn in life, or are weak, or have some dark mark on their karmic soul. Or perhaps their families are to blame, or society, or maybe life itself, for surely, something is to blame.

And so I looked everywhere to find reasons why, believing that if I could just find some answers there would be relief.

I'd read all those wonderful books written by physicists about the New Age: Gary Zukav, Fritjof Capra, Heinz Pagels. I was an enlightened person; I should be able to hold this as part of the cosmic scheme of life. But the suicide of my son had left me bereft and in pain. It is so easy to talk about faith and enlightenment. I was finding it a hell to live. Daily I forced myself to be open to the questions in hopes they would reveal some new door to understanding.

A phrase in Gary Zukav's book about the soul helped. "When we close the door to our feelings, we close the door to the vital currents that energize and activate our thoughts and actions."[10] I had to purposely work to keep the door to my feelings open, for I've never been good at expressing those emotions of sadness or anger. I grew up in a household that allowed for neither.

My children and friends were a safe haven. However, the "world" was not as safe. The attitude of society in general carried a stigma affecting not only the one who had committed suicide, but the family and loved ones as

---

[10]   Zukav, p. 60

well. That attitude keeps the problem of suicide hidden. Kay Jamison, in her book *Night Falls Fast*, writes "What we do not know kills."[11]

The reality of this was brought home to me as I moved back into my work. I began to read beneath the comments and looks from others. I saw the furtive glances of those who knew me only slightly. From some I fended off crude comments. "Was it drugs?" a woman asked. "Maybe it was AIDS," said another. I felt overwhelmed at trying to explain to people I hardly knew, and I was saddened as I saw the condemnation of my son. The "mother tiger" in me rose to defend him and us.

A fall had left me with two fingers of my right hand badly injured. The doctor had prescribed physical therapy and I had struck up a casual friendship with the young therapist who was treating me at the hand clinic. Eventually, she asked the usual questions about my marital state, my work, and family. "How many children do you have?" she asked. Automatically, I replied, "Four," and then gasped. I didn't know if I should say four or three.

She frowned. "Did I hurt you?"

"No," I said. "It's just that one of my children is dead."

She was sympathetic and asked the dreaded question. "What happened?"

In the few moments before my reply, a hundred thoughts flashed through my mind. I saw I didn't want to deal with her attitude and opinions about suicide, and most of all, I didn't want the risk of having her condemn my son—even in her thoughts. I was shocked, for in other areas of my life I'm straightforward and have no trouble telling the truth. But in this instance, I was cowardly. "I don't like to talk about it. It brings back such sad memories," I said. She was understanding and pressed the subject no further, but I was faced with the reality of that issue—society's opinion about my son and his family because of his suicide.

I had to find out why we as a society had this attitude. My first stop was the dictionary. My *Webster's Collegiate Dictionary* said, according to use in 1643 "suicide: noun . . . the act or an instance of taking one's own life voluntarily and intentionally especially by a person of years of discretion and of sound mind; one that attempts suicide." According to usage from 1773 on, "adjective . . . of or relating to suicide: esp: being or performing a deliberate act resulting in the voluntary death of the person who does it." Then in 1841, it's a verb, ". . . suicide; suicided; suiciding: to commit

---

[11] Jamison, p. 19

suicide; to put oneself to death."[12] This was no help. Suicide was not only an act, but also a description of the individual who took his/her own life. My heart chilled. Was Bill *not* to be remembered for who he was, but for what he *did*?

By chance I came across the book *The Savage God: A Study of Suicide* by A. Alvarez. He tells that after his unsuccessful suicide attempt the London police (for suicide was considered a criminal offense in England) asked him questions they really didn't want answers to. "It was an accident, wasn't it, sir?" Alvarez, in his weakened state, agreed and the relieved officers quickly left.[13] After his survival, Alvarez began a personal study of the history and attitudes about suicide and came to the conclusion there could not be a single answer to such an ambiguous and complex act. As I read, I began to understand more about why we think about suicide the way we do.

Many cultures have revered those individuals who knowingly went to their death: Vikings, Druids, many African tribes, Indian *suttee*, Iglulik Eskimos, Kamikaze pilots, the Jews of Masada. Incas and Mayas killed themselves by the thousands to avoid being enslaved by the Spanish. Neither the Old Testament nor the New prohibit suicide. The Old Testament records the suicide of four individuals: Samson, Saul, Abimelech, and Achitophel. The New Testament records the suicide of Judas as being the proper action.

Early Greek literature is filled with examples of honorable suicides: Oedipus's mother Jocasta was considered a heroine for killing herself as a way out of an insufferable position; Aegus threw himself into the sea (which now bears his name—Aegean); Erigone hanged herself from grief. The suicides were allowed as long as they showed no wanton disrespect to the gods. Classical Greek suicide was dictated by a calm reasonableness. These were the Greek precepts for suicide: "Whoever no longer wishes to live shall state his reasons to the Senate, and after having received permission shall abandon life. If your existence is hateful to you, die: if you are overwhelmed by fate, drink the hemlock. If you are bowed with grief, abandon life. Let the unhappy man recount his misfortune, let the magistrate supply him with the remedy, and his wretchedness will come to an end."[14]

Tertullian, an early Pope, regarded Jesus' death as a form of suicide—that he had chosen death. Little attention was paid to suicide in those days, as

---

[12]   Merriam-Webster, p. 1249

[13]   Alvarez, p. 299

[14]   Ibid., p. 79

it was so common. Only slaves and soldiers were denied the right to kill themselves as they were considered to be property.

During the Sixth Century, St. Augustine changed that attitude. Taking his ideas from Plato's *Phaedo*, he reasoned that Christianity was founded on the belief that the human body housed the soul. This soul, which was to be judged in the next world, was immortal, thus making it not only equal to all other souls, but valuable as well. Life is a gift from God. To reject life is to reject God and to frustrate his will; to kill this image is to kill God. As a result of his writings, the Church inflicted the consequences of eternal damnation upon the one committing suicide.

In 533 A.D., the Council at Orleans decided that those who committed suicide were denied funeral rites. By A.D. 693, the Church decreed that those attempting suicide were excommunicated and thus assigned to the fires of hell. Those early Christian fathers took the rules even further. The body of the individual who had committed suicide was taken to a place of punishment and shame. There, the body was hanged on a gibbet, and no one could take the body down except by the authority of the magistrate. Then the body was usually buried at a crossroads. A stone was placed over the dead man's face and a stake driven through his heart. That guaranteed that the individual was condemned to forever roam and never find his way to heaven.

To add even greater harm, the name of the person was to be defamed *ad perpetuam rei memoriam*—for eternity. In England, suicides were considered to be felons and all their property was handed over to the crown. Their shields were broken, their woods cut, and their castles demolished. These laws lasted in England until 1870, and until 1961 an unsuccessful suicide could be sent to prison.

What nonsense, I thought. These brutal rules had done nothing to stop the suicides and had left the remaining family not only with their grief, but destitute as well.

John Donne, the famous English Anglican cleric and poet, seriously contemplated suicide as a young man. He wrote the first English defense of suicide, *Biathanatos*, showing that the ultimate moral problems of life, death, and responsibility were complex and open to question. The young Donne wrote, "I have often such a sickely inclination . . . Whensoever any affliction assailes me, mee thinks I have the keyes of my prison in mine owne hand, and no remedy presents it selfe so soone to my heart, as mine own sword. Often Meditation of this hath wonne me to a charitable interpretation of their action, who dy so."[15] In his later years, he found the book to be an embarrassment, but he didn't destroy it. He merely requested it be published posthumously.

We are still stuck in the attitudes that make suicide an anathema. And yet, the suicides continue. Kay Jamison claims that suicides among the young have tripled in the last forty-five years. It's the third leading cause of death in young people in the United States and second for college students. She graphed the number of deaths during the years of the Vietnam War (1960-1973) in males under the age of 35 for war deaths, HIV/AIDS, and suicide. The war took a terrible toll (54,708), but after twelve years it was over. During the same time period there were almost twice as many suicides (101,732).[16] When she compared the deaths from HIV with suicide, again the deaths from suicide were greater. The epidemic of HIV has not ended, but has slowed considerably. However, suicide continues unabated. Soldiers returning from combat are highly at risk. Every year over 36,000 Americans kill themselves, and over half a million make a suicide attempt medically serious enough to require emergency room treatment.[17]

Edwin Schneidman, an authority on suicide, claims it is difficult to get accurate numbers for research because of societies' attitudes about suicide. As I read, I felt overwhelmed. Back in the 1950s and 1960s I had been concerned about civil rights. There were things I could do about that, and I did them. But what could I do about this issue of the public attitude about suicide? I had no idea.

---

[15]   Donne, p. 8

[16]   Jamison, p. 22

[17]   Ibid., p. 24

Chapter Fourteen

As I continued to read books on suicide, I gained more insight into the individuals who had been driven to such a dramatic end. Understanding began to seep through the lines and words, vivid descriptions of the hell of depression. *Oh my God*, I thought, *could this have been what was troubling Bill?*

I knew nothing about depression, not the kind they called "clinical." I'd had my share of "blue days," but a father who had studied the philosophies of Bertrand Russell and Alfred White Northhead had raised me. He believed strongly in mind over matter. To those philosophers, the idea of a subconscious was considered "subversive." My father, so sweet and loving, never complained and detested tears. Under my father's tutelage, I had long ago learned to "suck it up." He had adored my husband, the son he never had, and it broke his heart when he saw what drinking did to Dick. He was sure that if Dick would just try harder he could throw off the bonds of demon rum. My father never accepted the idea that alcoholism was a disease. But I had freed myself from those old beliefs and was open to learn.

As I examined my son's life, I couldn't find any circumstantial evidence to support his suicide. A chance comment led me to the family tree and there I followed the bloodlines, Dick's and mine. I didn't document the stories of the many suicides in our families no one had dared mention before, as there were too many. Often reasons were given; excuses like soft comforters on a cold night, to help ease the pain or let someone "off the hook." Nerves, drinker, humped back, spinster, melancholic. It was obvious we carried within us a lethal disease. Was this hereditary?

Gradually it began to dawn on me that my son had suffered from clinical depression and I wept. He had cleverly hidden the symptoms. Again I had to ask his forgiveness for my ignorance and for society's arrogantly moralistic attitude toward the suicidal. For between the two, ignorance and arrogance, lay no hope for any help.

I find no nobility in pain and suffering. Too often, upon that individual who suffers are added the cruel attitudes of society. We make little distinction between depression (spelled with a small 'd') and clinical depression (which should be spelled with a big 'D'). We all have had those times when we were depressed; when everything seemed to be going all wrong. You were blue, felt depressed.

The blues cannot even come close to the agony of clinical depression. This kind of depression is not only more violent than schizophrenia, it is more common. About 6% of our population, approximately 15,000,000 people, are suffering. Jon Franklin writes, "Such depression, having no logical rationale for its existence, classically metamorphoses into self-hatred. It then becomes one of the most painful conditions known to man."[18] He goes on to explain that this psychic pain is more excruciating than kidney stones.

That helped explain why Bill would write in his suicide letter that his family would be better off without him. My heart ached as I thought of that. How I longed to hold him and tell him how wonderful he was; how loved by his family, respected and admired by his friends and co-workers. But it was too late for that.

I couldn't even begin to imagine what the pain of a clinical depression was. When there is an obvious reason—death of a loved one, loss of a job, divorce—one expects a certain amount of feeling depressed. However, when there is no obvious cause, as in the case with my son, the individual experiences a kind of self-hatred. William Styron describes it brilliantly in his book *Darkness Visible: A Memoir of Madness*. Styron was on his way to Paris to receive one of the highest awards given to a writer when he was struck with a bout of depression. He described it as being cast into the darkest pit of Hell from which he could see no help, no hope.

Scientists have made great advances in their understanding of the human brain, and educators and psychologists have learned much about human behavior. But we still have far to go to be understanding and appropriate in our dealings with one another. Recent research has shown that depression and alcoholism have nothing to do with will power or moral fiber, but our attitudes about them die slowly. We, as a society, still believe "they" could do something about it if they would only just try; or cared enough; or loved us; or changed jobs, companions, cities; etc. "Snap out of it," we say. They would if they could, but the snapper is broken.

---

[18] Franklin, p. 18

Boris Pasternak, in an epitaph for all the Russian poets who had died by their own hand, wrote "To start with what is most important: we have no conception of the inner torture which precedes suicide . . . What is certain is that they all suffered beyond description, to the point where suffering has become a mental sickness. And, as we bow in homage to their gifts and to their bright memory, we should bow compassionately before their suffering."[19]

Alvarez, who had failed in his attempt to kill himself, wrote, "A suicidal depression is a kind of spiritual winter, frozen, sterile, unmoving. The richer, softer and more delectable nature becomes, the deeper that internal winter seems, and the wider and more intolerable the abyss which separates the inner world from the outer. Thus suicide becomes a natural reaction to an unnatural condition."[20]

I was sure my mother had suffered from depression, a cyclical darkness that came always before the months of spring, or on those days when the sun stayed hidden. My father traveled and we lived out in the country, on a lovely lake. I'm sure my mother was lonely, for my sister and I were involved in our school activities and friends. Mother is now dead and my heart ached for her and for me—all the missed opportunities where I could have shown more compassion.

The genetic and chemical links to depression, alcoholism, schizophrenia, and other mental ills have been uncovered. When the scientific community realized the physical basis for these illnesses, they collected the chains and shackles from mental institutions, had them melted down, and cast into a bell. This bell hangs at the National Mental Health Association in Arlington, Virginia. When I learned this, tears filled my eyes for I realized we could, as a society, grow in our knowledge and understanding.

But public opinion changes slowly, and psychiatric dogma has reduced progress to a crawl. Most practitioners in the twentieth century held that mental illness was invariably caused by environmental factors: poor mothers, abusive fathers, etc. The reports of some possible dangerous side effects of drugs fueled the conflict between talk-therapists and drug-therapists. The idea of the "soap opera" aspect of life is tantalizing, and so the gossip and stories spread of why people behave as they do. One need merely read the newspaper or turn on TV news to hear reporters give their opinions on the

---

[19] Alvarez, pp. 268-9
[20] Ibid., p. 103

reasons for people's actions. And read the obituary columns. The same old phrases are used to give us reasons for why people die. It seems our society desperately needs to have a cause and the more dramatic, the better.

Religions and other institutions have used the fears of sin, excommunication, and rejection to try to keep individuals from committing that act of self-murder. Journalists write condescendingly of suicides, as if the reporter is somehow stronger and better than the one committing the deed. I was outraged when I read the report of the death of Mrs. W. Mark Felt. "It was suicide, not a heart attack, that felled his [W. Mark Felt's] wife after years of strain from Felt's FBI career and ensuing legal troubles."[21] I wanted to shout out, "Who said so?" Had she left a note saying that? Why give a reason at all?

The language of people on the street is filled with Freudian jargon about "those" people. And everyone has an opinion as to why the person committed suicide.

I'd been guilty of using that jargon myself. I'd grown up in a society that believed that the person who commits suicide is weak and cowardly, a failure in life and disgrace to the family. But not one of the suicides in our family tree had been weak or a failure. How could they be condemned as weak? Each one had overcome the strongest natural urge we are born with—to stay alive.

Not only does society in general condemn the person committing suicide, along with the family, but also those organizations and institutions that should give solace often pull back as if fearing contamination. Once the funeral is finished, you're on your own. Therapists are expensive and not a panacea. James Howe, president of the National Alliance for The Mentally Ill, complains that too many psychiatrists and psychologists still refuse to recognize the limitations of talk therapy.[22] The problem is that although it is extremely effective with some individuals, it doesn't work with others and it doesn't work predictably. And when it doesn't work, too often the patient is left believing he or she was the cause of the failure.

I know that Bill and Laura had gone to a therapist, a good one, and she had seen no problem other than Bill should communicate more. When I heard that I wanted to throttle her. I was sure that Bill would have communicated more if he could have.

---

21 *The Seattle Times,* April 23, 2006, p. A9

22 Franklin, p. 268

As an educational therapist, I've worked with dozens of children and adults who seemed to have difficulty, and some even an inability, to translate their feelings into language. The problem often showed up in their trouble with reading comprehension. They simply could not interpret the subtle inferences of stories into words, particularly those involving feelings and emotions.

As a young child, my son seemed unable to tell us how he felt about things, one of the symptoms of clinical depression. Whenever asked, he'd say everything was "fine" or "okay." I didn't know then about the language of art and movement, but we communicated non-verbally. Bill drew great comfort from his artistic expression. His computer greeting cards (some six feet long) were filled with grace and whimsical humor. His intricate mobiles show a dynamic balance of light and darkness. There was no question that he loved his family. He manifested his deep feelings outwardly. There was no clue to the depression he suffered inwardly.

Many individuals, unable to express themselves directly about their pain (and that is the nature of depression) do so in their art and writings. Anthony Storr writes, "In a recent study of forty-seven British writers and artists, selected for eminence by their having won major awards or prizes . . . 38% had been treated for affective illness. Poets were particularly subject to severe mood-swings, and no less than half the sample studied had been treated with drugs as out-patients, or admitted to hospitals for treatment with anti-depressants, electroconvulsive therapy, or lithium."[23]

Among those poets, writers, and artists who, over history, have suffered from depression were: Keats (from whom Alvarez borrowed the term "The Savage God" for the title of his book on suicide), Traherne, Wordsworth, Byron, Hart Crane, Robert Lowell, Van Gogh, Virginia Woolf, Modigliani, Gorki, Sylvia Plath, Jackson Pollack, Ernest Hemingway, and Rainer Maria Rilke. It was obvious that abilities and success could not stop bouts of depression.

As I looked through our family albums I saw Bill, a beautiful child who began having dark moods. Even at four years of age there was the occasional picture of a little boy who looked as if he were lost in some gloomy thought. I was filled with feelings of rage. *If only I'd known*, I thought. But that kind of thinking led to nowhere but despair. I read Rilke's poem again and opened myself to face the next questions. It would be easier to just bury myself in denial, but I knew I would continue to question. Bill would have wanted that.

---

[23]   Storr, p. 142

Chapter Fifteen

I read these books as a layperson. I had no desire to pursue the science. I only wanted to understand, to see if there was anything that could help assuage the pain of his loss. I often felt I was way over my head, but I labored on, like paddling a canoe upstream, sure that somewhere I would stumble on answers that would comfort me.

I enjoyed reading Jon Franklin's book *Molecules of the Mind*. He took a difficult subject and made it not only interesting, but also easy to understand. One of his comments gave me an "Aha!" moment. On page eighteen of his book, he wrote that psychic pain is located in the brain. A new field for me to investigate.

My background in science is limited, but I plunged into this new area, dictionary close at hand. The readings gave me little comfort other than to know that scientists were working to find answers to some of the baffling questions around why we are the way we are. I came away feeling we are still in the dark ages about how our minds work

Richard Restak wrote, "Traditionally, psychiatrists have separated mental illness into disorders of *thinking* and *emotion*. We now know that these distinctions are largely artificial, that the brain cannot be so neatly compartmentalized. Disturbed thoughts produce disturbed emotions, and vice versa."[24]

Then I struggled with a book written by Candace Pert, *Molecules of Emotion: The Science Behind Mind-Body Medicine*. While still a doctoral candidate, she and Michael Kuhar mapped the chemical brain, locating the electrical activity in the brain centers that process psychological pain. These psychic centers had evolved from more basic physical pain centers and apparently use the same receptors. Perhaps the psychic balance between elation and depression is

---

[24]   Restak, p. 295

controlled by the bodies' natural morphine system, the endorphins released during the common "runner's high." These endorphins give us a sense of feeling good about ourselves. Pert and Kuhar also discovered that the levels of cortical releasing factor (CRF) almost always show a tenfold higher level in the cerebrospinal fluid of those who kill themselves compared to those who died from other causes.[25] When this CRF hits the pituitary gland, it stimulates the secretion of ACTH, a stress hormone. When ACTH hits the adrenal glands, it manufactures the steroid corticosterone. Stress increases with increased steroid production. Pert believes that depressed people are in a chronic state of ACTH activation because of a disrupted feedback loop that fails to signal when there are sufficient levels of steroid in the blood.

The normal brain, even after having its morphine receptors stimulated artificially, can return to the normal flow of the "good-feeling" endorphin, that natural morphine-like chemical the body produces. However, some brains cannot. The scientists suggest there may be several causes for this, but regardless of the reasons, the victims can never feel good about themselves. They remain in constant psychological pain.

I put the books aside and wept. They were informative, but did not appease my grief. And a new question was forming. I was quite sure my son had suffered from depression. And I knew he had first entertained the idea of suicide when he was only eight years old. Surely others had thought of suicide when they were young and had given it up. But not my son. Why had he continued this personal conversation about suicide?

---

[25]   Pert, p. 270

Chapter Sixteen

I was haunted by the question of why my son had committed suicide. But now, with the poem Bill had left us, I was reading in a new way, more willing to live with ambiguity, open to all kinds of answers and settling on none.

In Gazzaniga's book *Nature's Mind: The Biological Roots of Thinking, Emotions, Sexuality, Language, and Intelligence* he used the word *psychoneuroimmunology* which is the study of the interaction of the mind (psycho), the nervous system (neuro), and the immune system (immunology). This made great sense to me and I began to see how delicately they are all interrelated.

Then I found Gary Marcus's book *The Birth of the Mind*. He suggested that we *think* we think in words, however, the scientific community is divided on this subject. Some say there is a slippage between language and thought, for there are thoughts we can't find words for. There can be thoughts without language, but not that language plays no role in thought. Babies, monkeys, and aphasics (adults who have lost their ability to speak) all have thoughts, even if they cannot speak. We all have thoughts that we can't put into words—emotions, sensations, and so forth—but that shows only that *some* thoughts are not linguistic, not that *no* thoughts are.[26]

The scientific books proved to be difficult and offered little comfort. And so I turned to books of philosophy and spirit. One from India called the mind a "drunken monkey." I could relate to that for I knew what little control I had over my thinking.

In the 1960s, Maxwell Maltz, a plastic surgeon, wrote *Psycho-Cybernetics: A New Technique for Using Your Subconscious Power*. Step-by-step he showed how changing your thinking will improve your self-image. Then in the 1970s, physicists began writing about their work in ways the layperson (like

---

26   Marcus, pp. 125-126

me) could understand. Some examples: Gary Zukav's *The Dancing Wu Li Masters;* Heinz Pagels' *The Cosmic Code*; Fritjof Capra's *The Tao of Physics* and *The Turning Point*. At the same time, Western writers were introducing the thinking of Eastern philosophers in a way that the layperson could grasp. Allan Watts was one of the first. Then Thaddeus Golas with *The Lazy Man's Guide to Enlightenment* and Shakti Gawain's *Creative Visualization.* I remember when I read them I felt my heart sing. They all made great sense. I was "enlightened" enough to be able to understand the flow of life—of karma, Kismet, the interesting questions of philosophy. But on the day death came into my life, when I learned that my son was dead, it was no longer mere academic "play." Now I needed to *live* the understanding I had gained. A very different game.

I was deluged with bits of wisdom. They were everywhere—those simplistic aphorisms of how to be happy. Jonathan Haidt, in his book *The Happiness Hypothesis,* claims the mind is divided into parts that sometimes conflict. He claims we are like a rider on the back of an elephant and we think we're in control. Sometimes the elephant goes off in its own direction. I definitely could relate to that.

My doctoral work had taken me to books about language. One could spend a lifetime in its study. I now believe that *language* played its part, just as the depression did, in my son's choice to die.

Language can affect our thoughts in two ways: One is by framing or focusing our thinking much like a flashlight points our attention in a certain way. Henry Kissinger cleverly said, "Mistakes were made." In speaking that way he avoided the embarrassment of saying *who* made the mistakes. The spin-doctors know that to frame a sentence is to focus a thought in a particular direction.

The other way language is used is in what we remember. Gary Marcus uses the example of a computer. Its memory is made up of a long string of "bits" that can be either zeros or ones which mean nothing without an organizational theme. Perhaps we are *encoding* our experiences in special ways in our long-term memory banks. I am often surprised when at family gatherings my sister relates a family incident. My recall differs from hers and if I say that, she always says, "Are you sure?" Of course I am—as sure of my memory as she is of hers. What a peculiar thing is the mind. Richard Dawkins claims it's not a blueprint, more of a recipe for baking. Once baked, the cake cannot be broken down again into its components—this crumb matches the first word in the recipe, etc. We think we are recalling an incident much as if we were re-showing a video. But it doesn't work like that. Scientists know very little about the mechanisms by which memories are retrieved. Neural pathways for memory are not found in one particular location in the brain, but are spread throughout, with different circuits supporting different kinds of memory. There's one spot for sound, another for color, and so forth. We are pulling that memory out bit by bit. Our memories are "iffy" at best and memories that are painful or frightening are deeply embedded.

What was my son focusing on? What was he remembering? How was that affecting his life? Had that led to his suicide? What kind of internal conversations was he having? I had nothing but questions.

Chapter Seventeen

Many people at some time or other have thought about suicide only to give up the idea and never think of it again. Our city streets and parks are filled with individuals for whom all hope is gone. They are homeless, often addicted, alone. And yet they live on, the thought of suicide foreign to them.

However, among some individuals this thought regarding "ending it all" becomes a private conversation they have with themselves. For some the conversation becomes all-consuming and relief is found only in committing the deed. What makes the difference?

I believe that for my son the thought of suicide started when he was young and became an obsession. An English novelist who made two serious suicide attempts said, "I don't know how much potential suicides think about it. I must say, I've never really thought about it much. Yet it's always there. For me, suicide's a constant temptation. It never slackens. Things are all right at the moment. But I feel like a cured alcoholic: I daren't take a drink because I know that if I do I'll go on it again. Because whatever it is that's there doesn't alter. It's a pattern of my entire life."[27]

This act of suicide could be seen as an act of exorcism, the exorcism of the death thought.

"But," you could argue, "why didn't he just look at the circumstances around him and see how worthwhile he was and how successful?" William Styron, a successful author, writes of his bout with depression. "I felt loss at every hand. The loss of self-esteem is a celebrated symptom, and my own sense of self had all but disappeared, along with any self-reliance."[28]

---

[27]   Alvarez, p. 124

[28]   Styron, p. 56

We don't know what Bill was "seeing." We did not know his thoughts, nor does it matter what the circumstances were. He had a certain perspective of his life. We all do. We all *know* how things are. We know *how* we are. In a workshop on self-esteem, I have the participants make a list describing themselves. "I am . . ." Then I have them write down who said so. Often, they are amazed, for they are still acting out a scenario given them long ago, which is no longer appropriate. A friend of mine finally realized in her middle forties that she was still dressing the "cute" little girl she had been throughout her youth. What a difference that realization meant for her!

We all have a silent listener at our side. It's been there all of our lives, perhaps even before we were born. It's our subconscious mind. It has no feelings and no opinions. It merely obeys. It's like the disk used to make a master record. It records everything. Under hypnosis, people are able to recall sounds, smells, feelings—everything. Then to complicate things even further we keep making sense out of the information we're taking in. For example, when my granddaughter Megan was three, she proudly told me a factory was where you made horses. Nothing I said could dissuade her. Several days later, we took a ride in the country. "See, Grammy," she said, pointing out of the window. There it was, an abandoned factory, its tall smokestack jutting into the sky, and there surrounding it were all the horses.

Isn't that cute, I thought. Then I realized that's what we do—we use our perceptions to make sense out of everything. The consequences may not be as cute as Megan's. When I was married, cameras were not allowed in the sanctuary. So I went to a photographer before the wedding to have my portrait taken. When my husband-to-be was looking at the proofs, he asked, "Why didn't you have a profile made?"

"With my big nose!" I said.

He frowned and took me to a three-way mirror. To my great surprise I saw that my nose is rather small. I had been looking in mirrors my entire life and my eyes had not changed what my mind thought—that my nose was big. Who knows how I put all that together. The point is I did and *lived my life as if it were so.*

I'm not the only one. A friend called me one day all excited. "I'm not small!" he said.

I laughed for I knew he was six feet tall, certainly not small.

Then he told me that while out of town, he'd gone to see one of the adventure films his wife hates. The movie was already in progress when he arrived and the only seating was in the front row. He tiptoed in the dark to his seat. As he looked up, the screen was filled with the image of a man. A memory flooded Jim's mind and he remembered an incident from his youth. He'd done something he wasn't supposed to do and had sneaked into his bedroom and closed the door. His dad had come home and innocently opened the bedroom door and spoke to his son. Jim was seated on the floor and when he looked up at the giant in the doorway he *knew* that he was small and powerless. That decision directed his actions in his life. As he realized this in the theater, Jim said he began to weep and felt a rush go through his body as if releasing something. "I feel like a new man," he said.

A friend told me that just recently her first love, who had abruptly ended their relationship, told her he'd left her because he loved her too much. He feared, at age seventeen, that they'd get married and he'd spend his life working at a service station to support them. This was twenty years after the event, but it changed her entire life. She had always assumed that he'd left because he didn't love her. The years she had spent feeling abandoned and not loved disappeared.

These decisions we make about ourselves—big nose, too small, abandoned—are personal. Someone may have said, "You're such a klutz!" But when you think of yourself, you do not think, "You are a klutz." No. You think "*I am . . .*" We personalize those thoughts. I call them the "Tape." We all have one. The tragedy of the Tape is that the comments are usually negative—subtle and not-so-subtle put-downs and criticisms.

Julian Jaynes writes of "excerpting" information about ourselves.[29] He explains that we can only see or pay attention to a part of a thing at any moment. Think of a circus. Or a city. Or yourself. You will excerpt parts of the circus, parts of the city, parts of yourself, not the things themselves. You are aware of things as you perceive them to be. And you will act out of that perception. The belief I had about my nose being big is a perfect example of that. I could not have a profile of my face for I *knew* I had a big nose.

If, when you think of the circus, you excerpt the color, excitement, and fun, you are liable to want to go see one. If, however, you thought of the danger, the long drive, the expense, heat, and possibility of harm, you will not be interested.

Well, you say, just change your attitude about the circus. Not so easy to do. The excerptions are based on your interpretations and perceptions

---

[29] Jaynes, pp. 61-62

of *what is so*. And they are *real*. Try changing that painful memory from your youth. In many cases, your body may still react in the way it did when the event first occurred. To try to change the neural pathways by pretending, or saying affirmations, is an exercise in folly. Basic changes can be made, but they either are dramatic, like conversion experiences, or require a disciplined effort over time.

Recovering alcoholics are an example. For some, it will happen as it did for Dr. Bill, co-founder of Alcoholics Anonymous. His many attempts to control his drinking had always ended in failure. "No words can tell of the loneliness and despair I found . . . I had been overwhelmed. Alcohol was my master."[30]

After a visit from a friend who had overcome alcohol by turning his life and will over to a power greater than himself, Dr. Bill very simply did the same. He writes, "These were revolutionary and drastic proposals, but the moment I fully accepted them, the effect was electric. There was a sense of victory, followed by such a peace and serenity, as I had never known. There was utter confidence. I felt lifted up, as though the great clean wind of a mountaintop blew through and through. God comes to most men gradually, but His impact on me was sudden and profound."[31] Dr. Bill never had another drink. His doctor was amazed. Something had happened that he didn't understand. For others the change is gradual. Individuals spend their lives daily surrendering to a power greater than themselves. "Easy does it." "One day at a time." These are the mantras they live by.

Our ability to make these changes is somewhat dependent on what's going on in our brains. The neuroscientists claim that thoughts emerge from the complex interactions of large numbers of individual neurons. If the chemistry of the brain is changed, thinking changes. The brain under the influence of LSD didn't imagine the moon spoke. It *knew* the moon spoke and *heard* the words spoken.

One of my graduate students, a nurse named Mary, told me that as a child she had been a good girl and an excellent student. Her report card always showed all A's. When she was thirteen, her family moved and she went to a new school. Within a few months, her A's had dropped to F's and the formerly friendly little girl was now sullen and miserable. The school

---

[30]   Alcoholics Anonymous, p. 8

[31]   Ibid., p. 14

counselor began to treat Mary for psychological problems and hinted to her parents the behavior may be due to drugs or parental abuse.

Mary's parents were desperate and went to a doctor. His cursory examination found nothing wrong and he blamed puberty and the angst of being a teenager in a new school for the problems.

A trip to their former home included a visit with Mary's former teacher. "There is something wrong with this child," she said. Now fortified, Mary's mother returned to the doctor and like a squeaky wheel made enough noise to get the attention needed. Mary's thyroid was the problem. An operation removed two-thirds of it. She was placed on medication and after a short recovery period returned to school. Her grades went back to A's and her sunny disposition quickly returned. The chemistry of Mary's body had dramatically affected not only her behavior, but her thinking as well. Each individual had seen Mary's problems through their disciplines—what they *knew* to be the truth. The teacher saw Mary was having trouble making friends. The doctor saw her as a typical teenager, rebellious and recalcitrant. The psychologist was sure it was mental problems. Only the parents kept asking the question until the proper answer was found.

Gregory Bateson claims you cannot separate what a person is, the world he lives in, from how he knows about his world. "His (commonly conscious) beliefs about what sort of world it is will determine how he sees it and acts within it, and his ways of perceiving and acting will determine his beliefs about its nature."[32]

If, in this intricate, delicately balanced system called the brain, any small portion is changed, thinking and perception can change. I believe that suicide is a private conversation an individual has with him/herself. That conversation, added to a physical/biological imbalance in the brain, can become an obsession, a mantra repeated over and over, that even the strongest find impossible to resist. Death at least stills the thought.

---

[32]   Bateson, p. 314

Chapter Eighteen

We think in language, in words, and our first experience with words was hearing them spoken. We learned when very tiny the power of the voice of the parent to approve or disapprove. As small children we found the influence and potential for hurt and joy in words. Our lives are intricately woven with language, and there is a strong but subtle connection of words and sound. We "hear" the thoughts in our heads. We entertain those thoughts, conversing with ourselves. I see it all the time, people having conversations with themselves in their cars, at the market, walking down the street. I do it myself. We act as if there were a little person inside our heads, manufacturing thoughts with which we then engage. I find that as I wake in the mornings, my conversation is in full swing. Most of us have had those times we awakened in the middle of the night and tossed and turned, worrying over some issue—should I do X or how about Y? That worry was in words, in our thinking.

To hear someone speak, we have to suspend our own identities, even if only briefly, in order to listen. It's as if we must open a gate in our heads to let their words come in. How often have you been talking and realized the person you were speaking to "wasn't home?" They were not attending. To hear you, they had to set themselves—their agenda—aside.

The distance we maintain from one another is prescribed by our culture. We each have a personal "space," and when that space is invaded, we feel pressured or threatened. When a speaker is too close it feels as if he's trying to control our thoughts and we will step back. Only in a love relationship or with a close family member is a shorter distance comfortable.

To have someone speak closely to you, invade your personal space, and for you to remain listening, places that person in a psychological position of control. Now, imagine if the thought, in words like a voice, seemed to be coming from inside your own mind—more intimately than your most loving relationship. There is no way to elude the voice, no place to run to, nowhere to hide. Even if one uses drugs or alcohol to still the voice, there is always the letdown, the day after when the thought is not only there, but is more accusing than ever. There is no escape. One ends up believing the voice, obeying it, acting it out.

We are constantly judging, criticizing, and categorizing people. Our personal judgments of people help filter their influence over us. That is the easiest way to stay free from their dominance and control. For example, two boys are eating lunch in their middle school cafeteria. The school bully, much larger than either boy, enters and embarrasses one of the boys. When he leaves, the embarrassed boy says, "He's not so great," and what will follow is a "put-down." The private who mutters about his sergeant, "Your mother wears army boots," has found a way of diminishing the power exerted over him by the man whose rank is higher than his. How relieved we often are when we see the flaw in others. "They're no better than we are," we think.

Another powerful influence over us is the effect of station. My example: Two men are seated in a room. Each is at an identical desk. They are both wearing army camouflage uniforms. Each has three stripes on their sleeves. Man #1 says to Man #2, "Get me a cup of coffee."

Man #2 says, "Get it yourself."

Same room, same desks, same uniforms, only this time Man #1 is wearing bars on his shoulders. He says to Man #2, "Get me a cup of coffee."

Man #2 says, "Yes, sir."

This is not a matter of personality, for what "spoke" in the second example were the Major's bars. His position of authority spoke loudly. We sometimes forget the power some individual's words have had in our lives.

If the thought in your head is a put-down with an authoritative tone—"You're never going to make it!" "You're no good"—after a while, the strongest of us will succumb. Even if we counter-attack, the thought often seems to gather strength. How often have you, by yourself, with no outside help, dealt with a negative thought about yourself? The thought is more than words. It is actually a neurological pattern in your brain, one that gets stronger the more it is run. Even arguing against the negative thought reinforces the pattern.

Negative comments, especially when they come from someone in authority (and who has more authority than a parent), are as damaging as physical blows. The body recovers from the physical damage, but the mind keeps the negative comments and punishes the child throughout life. My elderly friends can still recite the "bad" things their mother or father said to them. It takes about ten positive comments to offset just one negative comment. I was once reviewing the assessments my students were required by law to fill out. Mine were reading very well, until I came to the sixteenth. This student did not like me, did not like the material, and hated the course. I was devastated. My whole body sagged in defeat. *That's it*, I thought. *I'm a lousy teacher*. Only later, as I forced myself to read them all and analyze what the assessments really were saying, did I realize that out of the forty graduate students, I had only one who hated me, four who thought I could have used more visuals, and thirty-five who thought my work was from okay to great. What did I concentrate on? The negative ones. They haunted me, like a condemnation. And they were my students. What if the comments had been from my boss? My parents? God?

William Styron, in his book *Darkness Visible,* wrote, "Of the many dreadful manifestations of the disease [depression], both physical and psychological, a sense of self-hatred—or, put less categorically, a failure of self-esteem—is one of the most universally experienced symptoms, and I had suffered more and more from a general feeling of worthlessness as the malady had progressed. My dank joylessness was therefore all the more ironic because I had flown on a rushed four-day trip to Paris in order to accept an award which should have sparklingly restored my ego."[33]

When I read those words I thought of Bill's suicide note—his claim that his family would be better off without him. My heart broke once more.

My son was in third grade when his thoughts about suicide began. It was at that time that my friend Peter committed suicide. He'd been a minister who'd lost his job teaching at a seminary for his beliefs were suspect to the traditional authorities there. Bill, at eight, was with me when I received the phone call telling of Peter's suicide. I don't remember what I told the children. I only know I told the truth and tried to explain as best I could. It was also at that age that Bill's father began making negative comments to him.

I knew little about suicide, had never personally known anyone who had committed suicide. I had only vague memories of the whispers of suicide in my mother's family—a great uncle, and a cousin twice removed. My aunts had discussed those deaths while they did the dishes after our family gatherings and we children had eavesdropped. It was the only way to find out about the mysteries of babies, marriage, and death.

---

[33] Styron, p. 5

Most suicides have the thought occur while in their teens or younger, a most vulnerable time, when the ego/self is still in the course of becoming. Who knows how old Sylvia Plath was when her "voices" first started. She reveals them clearly in these lines from her poem "Daddy."[34]

So, daddy, I'm finally through,
The black telephone's off at the root,
The voices just can't worm through.

I contend that suicide is a thought a person has, which then for internal and external reasons becomes obsessive, a mantra, which begins to shape his life. Alvarez writes, "Once a man decides to take his own life he enters a shut-off, impregnable but wholly convincing world where every detail fits and each incident reinforces his decision."[35] After Bill's death, the investigating detective told Doug that Bill had purchased the poison the week before Thanksgiving. That was the day Laura said he came home happy, his arms full of flowers. My psychologist friend Paul said it is common for the person contemplating suicide to feel the depression lift as soon as they've chosen their method of dying. And when the depression lifts they know they are on the right path—death.

Talk therapy and drug therapy may help, but only if the person is able to express how he feels, what he is thinking. If the person is unable to translate his feelings into words, and I believe this to be far more common than we realize, the therapy won't help. I think the person needs a support system of like-kind, much like the support alcoholics get in AA or their loved ones get in Alanon. This would enable them to surrender to the thought, no longer to fight with it, to have to excel in order to hide it. They'd be able to surrender to a Power greater than oneself, even if that power is an "I don't know." Too often these individuals cannot articulate in language what is happening for them, but there is a mutual "knowing" that transcends words and explanations. To be able to go to a meeting and say, "Hi, my name is Bill and I'm suicidal," and to have open accepting faces greet you with, "Hi, Bill," might be the first steps to bring the suicidal thoughts into the clear light of day. Taking these steps might lead to peace and eventual recovery.

---

[34] Plath, p. 76
[35] Alvarez, p. 144

Brendan Koerner writes that a new study of the brain shows that group therapy proved highly effective in treating posttraumatic stress disorder: 88.3% of the study's subjects who underwent group therapy no longer exhibited PTSD symptoms after completing their sessions, versus just 31.3% of those who had no contact with other sufferers.[36] Koerner's article also stated that the sharing in the AA groups enhanced self-awareness. Could there be a similar effect from a group of suicidal individuals? Perhaps some comfort in knowing you are not alone?

But for any of that to happen, we must allow the conversation of suicide to be open, and take it out of the moral light in which it is so often held. The organization Alcoholics Anonymous has not created more alcoholics. The self-help groups that deal with other addictions do not add to the problem in society. Talking about suicide openly does not cause bystanders to begin to think suicidal thoughts. On the contrary, it allows for those suffering to find a way to get some help.

That work is already beginning, and it has taken our young people to lead the way. In Washington state, with media messages designed by a group of students, the Youth Suicide Prevention Program began educating youth and adults about suicide. The teens visit schools and talk with students. Their website, www.yspp.org, receives hundreds of thousands of hits each year. And they are getting positive results.

Suicide is one of our most serious health/social problems and we must take the steps to deal with it. Bringing it out of the closet is one way to begin.

---

[36] Koerner, *TheWeek*, July 23, 2010

Chapter Nineteen

"You don't ever have to forgive him," a friend said one day at lunch.

I thanked him, for I knew he had spoken out of his concern for me. But I have forgiven, not only Bill, but myself as well. Not right away, for my pain was deep and needed to be healed from within, but I finally did, and I keep forgiving.

Forgiving is something we do in language. In my studies with Fernando Flores I learned about speech acts. These acts consist of requests and promises, assertions and assessments, and declarations.[37] The most powerful form of language is a declaration. Assertions require proof and assessments must be grounded or they are merely opinions. However, declarations require no proof, no history. The proof rests in the "declarer" and the action of that "declarer." The document that begins, "When in the Course of human events . . ."[38] is a powerful declaration. The men who wrote those words had little backing for such powerful statements. They had no proof democracy could work, no history. They may have felt unsure of themselves or wondered about what they were doing, but they made a declaration and lived that declaring. Today our actions keep that declaration alive—we, the people of the United States do that. For declarations exist only in the actions of the declarer. If we were to stop being a democracy, the declaration would vanish as if it had never been.

President Kennedy said that in ten years we would have a man on the moon. There was no history of anything like this, no proof that such a venture was even possible. But he was the President of the most powerful country in the world. Overnight, agencies were formed, scientists gathered and began

---

[37]   Winograd and Flores, pp.58-59

[38]   *The Declaration of Independence*

to work, and before the ten years was even over, two men walked on the face of the moon.

To forgive is a dynamic declaration. "To give up resentment against or the desire to punish; stop being angry with; pardon."[39] To say "I, because **I** say so, with no proof, do hereby forgive," is powerful. It changes your life.

Too often we wait to forgive someone, looking to see if they're worthy to be forgiven, or if they've "suffered" unforgiven long enough. But forgiveness has nothing to do with them, and everything to do with us. We are the ones harboring the feelings of resentment, regret, loss, and hurt.

To forgive doesn't necessarily mean to take back into your bosom, to go back as before. It may not be wise to do so. You may say, "I forgive you and I don't want to see you again," with no malice in your heart. The "don't want" comes out of wisdom not hatred; out of finally realizing it may not be smart to set yourself up again for another disaster. For life must go on and it can't if you are holding fast to a resentment. Those resentments dwell within you and each one weighs a thousand pounds. You are the one who'll get the wrinkles or the illness, not them. You are the one who will pay the price.

And so we forgave Bill and ourselves, each in our own way and own time. Although she knew in the light of day that she was not guilty for Bill's death or even his unhappiness, Laura spent some sleepless nights chastising herself for every little thing she'd done wrong. She finally went to see a good therapist. It took only one visit for Laura to realize that Bill meant what he wrote about loving her and its being a "privilege" to have known them. Because she knew that to be true she has never felt anger toward Bill.

Laura says she thinks of Bill often and mentions him to the boys. Laura's signal that Bill is with them is music. Several years after Bill's death, Spencer needed some important corrective eye surgery. As Laura drove into the parking lot of UCLA Medical Center, the Talking Heads song that Bill loved came on the radio. She and Bill had driven into that same parking lot when Spencer was two for his first eye surgery. It seemed as if Bill was letting her know he was with them, keeping them safe. She's grateful he was her first husband and father of her sons. He was a loving, caring father and she likes seeing his traits in the boys. Both sons are creative, handsome, with great senses of humor.

Laura had the school psychologist coach her on how to talk about the death with the boys. She had made a personal declaration that Bill's death

---

[39]   Merriam-Webster, p. 491

would strengthen her sons, not handicap them. To strengthen her stand, she took them to a psychologist. After five visits, the psychologist assured Laura that the boys were doing well and did not need future visits. They missed their dad terribly, as Bill and Laura had shared the responsibilities of caring for the children. For a long while after Bill's death, Laura and I slept with them. Alec was only two and had a hard time expressing his feelings or thoughts. In the six months following the death he went through a spell of temper tantrums. Laura consulted the counselor at his nursery school and found ways to help him learn to control his anger. We all assisted as best we could, but it was Laura who helped get him through that difficult time. Her strength and unwavering love gave both boys the safety they needed. Later, as an adolescent, Alec told Laura that he'd had a really tough time with his father's suicide when he was in fourth and fifth grades. Laura and Sandy kept trying to find ways to have conversations about Bill's death, but Alec didn't know how to talk about it. Finally at age sixteen, Alec took the Landmark Forum for Teens and had a huge breakthrough. During the seminar, the Forum Leader asked if anyone had had someone do something really thoughtless to them. Alec raised his hand. He and the Leader (who ironically knew Bill) had a powerful conversation about his father's death. She listened and encouraged Alec to go deep into his feelings and express them. That night he wrote a private letter to his dead father which allowed him to fully experience completion. At the close of the seminar, Alec thanked the Leader and let her know he was okay.

Spencer liked talking about his dad with me. He'd come and lean across my knee and ask a question about Bill. The conversations never took very long, but it was a tender way in which we touched each other—Spencer, Bill and me. Even at that young age he seemed to recognize that I was comforted when we talked, and his loving concern moved me deeply. At first, Spencer talked with me in a way he couldn't talk with his mother. He felt a strong need to protect her. But he soon overcame that and now discusses everything with her.

Bill's sons are dealing with his death as they go through life. Where they are now is "healthy." But as they enter into new phases of manhood, they will have to again face the fact that their father committed suicide. And we have no doubt they will do that and be supported in their efforts.

Sandy had been with Bill just two nights prior to his death. He was shocked at the news, and his first thought was, "If only I'd known he was in such turmoil and pain." Fortunately, a good friend was there to comfort

Sandy when he was told of the suicide. Later that night, Sandy went for a long walk and talked with Bill, thinking through the kind of conversation he and Bill could have had.

Several months later, Sandy found he was having some critical thoughts about Bill. At first he was surprised that he would think that way, but then put into perspective the kind of adulation he'd been feeling. He knew he needed to allow Bill to be the person he was—neither saint nor sinner. Those thoughts allowed Sandy to see how he'd not only forgiven Bill, but had also forgiven himself. "Bill was the kind of person who let his actions speak louder than words," Sandy said. "I don't think he could talk about himself." If Bill could have told Sandy his internal processes, he would have. And if Sandy had known, he would have responded appropriately. But "if only" conversations lead nowhere. Sandy doesn't entertain those thoughts.

This year when Sandy called me on Bill's birthday, I again thanked him for being such a good dad to my grandsons. He said he couldn't do it without Bill. "I check in with him about everything," he said.

Bill's brothers and sister went through their stages and came to forgiveness. John, the elder brother, had no difficulty forgiving Bill. It was forgiving himself that was the problem. He kept thinking he should have known something that would have helped, that he should have made one more phone call—should have done one more something. The fact that Bill's death was irreversible saddened John, and he had to deal with the absoluteness of death, but knowing that we are each ultimately responsible for ourselves, John finally forgave himself. He felt strongly that Bill did what he needed to do, even if we will never understand.

Mary feels in her heart that what Bill did was wrong, and she's sorry he abandoned his children. But she feels that in his mental state he did what he felt he had to do, so she has forgiven him and finds her love for him has not diminished in any way. She knows she's not Bill's judge, that he alone is responsible for his actions and for the consequences of those actions. She feels he's taking care of that now. How we deal with his dying affects our lives, not his. So Mary, in her heart, forgave Bill, and she lives that declaration daily.

Doug, so close to Bill in age, was the one who took care of us all. He's the one who identified Bill's body, made the arrangements for his cremation, found the site for his burial, and led the memorial. He never felt any anger toward Bill. He misses him, but has no resentment or anger. "We'll never know why," Doug told me. "Unless we lived in his body, thought his thoughts, perceived his perceptions, interpreted everything through him, there is no way to know. We could make up some reasons, but we will never know 'why' as far as Bill is concerned." Several times after Bill's death, Doug started to have the conversation "If only . . .," but he stopped himself each time. "I can't have that conversation," he told me. "There's no healthy place for it to go." Nothing can ever come from an "if only" kind of conversation. Those are daydreams, useful for creating stories and fairy tales. Doug realized he'd done the best he could, that he and Bill were friends, and there was nothing to do but to go on with life.

The declaration of forgiveness, requiring no proof, must be declared constantly, not in saying the words necessarily, but in the living of those words, being forgiving. What a joy it would be if you could forgive once, have it carved in granite, and be done with it, but it doesn't work that way. No proof, nothing material to refer to, to look at, touch, or see. It's like the paperweight my daughter gave me, a cube filled with a clear liquid and hundreds of red and silver stars. I shake it up and go back to my work, knowing the cube is filled with stars. Later, I look up and see that the cube is clear. Silently the stars sank while I was occupied.

It's like that with forgiving. I think it's all taken care of only to find some small incident or memory that reminds me again of the insanity of the deed or of my neglect. Just as action is required to make the stars in my paperweight float again, action is required to forgive.

To automatically say, "I forgive you," is unwise. There's no substance to it. Remember, this is a declaration and is valid only if the "declarer" is valid. I look at the memory and/or incident and experience what is there. Always there is an emotion, sometimes fear, or sadness, anger, or guilt. I find where it is located in my body and feel it, letting the feeling run its course. It doesn't work to intellectualize this in your mind! The feeling isn't there. You'll only rationalize and analyze and nothing will happen. Let the thoughts flow by, noticing them, but not doing anything with them. They're only thoughts. Let them go, along with the feelings. Imagine the thoughts and feelings draining out of you—through your fingers and toes as if they were taps you've opened. Because of the plasticity of our neural networks, new response patterns will develop, and eventually the old triggers will lose their impact.

"But how do you deal with the anger?" a friend asked. "Aren't you angry?"

Anger is a natural response, but it's a secondary emotion, always stemming from something else, usually loss. The loss of a loved one through rejection, and death is an irreversible rejection, will bring out anger. Don't stop at the anger. Look to see what's underneath, fueling it, and experience that.

When I once asked my mother how she felt about Bill's suicide, she smiled sweetly at me. "You know Uncle Sigmund's daughter Laura took her own life. But it's best not to talk about it," she said. "It's so sad." I never heard my uncle mention his daughter's death. However, several years after Bill's death, my mother said, "I think Bill was always affected by the death of his twin. After all, even though he was in your womb, he knew that child died, and he lived those months with that dead child." That was all she said, but it was enough to let me see that she had thought about the death and had done what she could to rationalize it. What she did with her feelings I don't know. As I said, she would never talk about it.

We live with a code of silence about such things, as if by not talking about them they will somehow disappear. I have no anger about that. My mother did the best she could, perfectly reflecting the culture in which she lived.

Chapter Twenty

To live with "if only" is to live a life that is doomed. There is no way to change the past; regretting it and feeling guilty about it do nothing to help in the present. We were all being quite successful in avoiding that conversation. However, the word "never" and the weight it carries had come up often in our thoughts and expressions. Never to see him again. Never to talk with him again. Never to hear his laugh. Never.

But I knew that in order to heal I had to face death in all its absoluteness, and hopefully someday accept the "never."

My thinking about that concept of "not ever again" expanded the world within which I live. The belief system I had built during my childhood was that we lived on earth and when we died our souls/spirits went on to "somewhere." Where, I wasn't sure, but never having to deal with death, I gave it little thought.

However, when it comes to the issue of spirits, I do have some notions. I won't call them beliefs, for beliefs are like answers in that they slam the door on inquiry, and I like to keep the question open and before me. If there is a "never," then there must be an "always." "Up" does not exist without "down." "Light" without "dark." Our world is dimensional. We live with time and space, the dead do not.

Our language is so limiting, so one-dimensional. The experiences we have are holistic, colorful, and filled with activity. Yet we are forced to describe them using words which trigger different meanings in each of us. And we must use these words in a logical, sequential manner, one after the other, in the hopes that our reader or listener is creating the kind of mental picture we mean to portray. Our words actually limit the width and breadth of experience, where our real living takes place. Philip Slater writes that the word explain, literally "ex-plain," means to *flatten out.*[40]

It is truly a miracle that we communicate at all. Writing of these experiences will be, according to Slater, like trying to portray the sun with a piece of string. My friend, the young priest Albert, called it ESP. He said he'd never seen such strong evidences of it in a family before. Perhaps, but I place no name on these experiences, nor any judgments.

Each of us, in our individual styles, sensed the drama that was unfolding. On that fateful March 2nd, I awakened at 5 am with a piercing headache; so severe I got out of my warm bed and took two aspirin. That was the hour Bill rose and left his house. My headache persisted throughout the day.

My daughter said that for three days before Bill's death she felt "horrible." She couldn't really describe the feeling, but said she didn't want to feel that way ever again.

Doug had called Bill at work the morning of March 2nd, something he had never done before.

My mother never called me. I always initiate the call. In ten years I'd probably had no more than six calls from her. But she called that afternoon, not knowing why. She just "felt" she should call.

My friend Patrick had arranged to come to Los Angeles to visit that weekend. His gentle understanding manner was exactly what I would need.

On the Sunday after Bill's death, I suddenly looked at the clock just as the digital numbers changed to 2:00. I felt something go through my body, like a murmur, then lift and leave. "He's free," I said aloud, not fully understanding what I said. It was three days since his death. I pictured Bill completing whatever initiatory rites on the other side, and wished him well on his new journey. I would miss him terribly, the wound in my heart there forever, but I would not hold him back. I would not only let him go, although everything in me wanted to cling to him, pull him back, keep him, I would wish him Godspeed, for love is letting go. I resolved I would learn to do as Rilke recommended—be patient toward all that is unsolved in my heart. In my state of numbness I had no idea how I could do that, but I was willing.

One night shortly after Bill's death, he came to me in a lucid dream. I knew I was dreaming and was awake in my dream state. Although I couldn't "see" him, I knew it was Bill. It seemed like he was surrounded by what I

---

[40] Slater, pp. 20-21

could only describe as "beings." They were all excited and joyously happy. Bill cupped my face in his hands and kissed me. "We're going to teach you to communicate with us directly," he said. "Are you willing?"

I was. And so began the lesson. I worked for what felt like hours until I was finally exhausted. "I'm sorry," I said. "I can't. It's like trying to move my eardrums. I don't even know where to start."

Bill laughed. "It's okay, Mom. We'll get through to you."

I have felt his presence often, we all do.

One afternoon, while working on this book, I suddenly began to cry. I left my computer and walked to my deck, weeping. I looked out over the Sound and said aloud, "I can't do this any more. The memories are so painful. It's too hard."

In the distance I saw a bird flying toward me. *That's an awfully big crow*, I thought. As it came closer, I saw it was an eagle flying directly toward me. An eagle! It had to swerve to avoid colliding with the building. Chills ran through my body. "Okay," I said aloud. "I get it." I walked back and continued writing.

The messages are everywhere in life, we merely need to be sensitive to them. Just as one can learn to tune in a short-wave radio, we can learn to tune in the subtle messages our loved ones are sending. As radios also build in protection from static and unwanted radio waves, we can learn to build in the protection devices so only that which is from the Light, from God, can get through.

Call it inspiration, right-brain thinking, imagination, creation, it really doesn't matter how you label the phenomenon. Just use it. We all have the capabilities of tapping into our own inner resources. We just need to start.

Bill had used his artistic abilities to send greetings and messages to his family and friends. He had decorated Mary's home when they had a graduation party for me. In a six-foot long banner over the front door were the words, "Congratulations, Dr. Mom." On the Valentine's Day before his death, he'd left his messages of love all over his house, tiny little red cardboard hearts. Laura found them everywhere; around her toothbrush, in the cupboard with the children's cereal, tucked into her date book. She said they kept surprising her all day.

In the weeks after Bill's death, I arrived one day to find Laura pale and shaken. "What's wrong?" I asked. She pulled her hand from her jacket pocket. In the palm were the tiny red hearts. I wasn't surprised, as I'd known about the Valentine heart caper.

"But, Ruth, this has been at the cleaners for months." I felt the familiar chill.

Laura left to run errands and I took Spencer and Alec out to the sidewalk so they could ride their little go-carts. I don't know how many trips they made back and forth. I only know I saw every inch of the pavement they covered. When it was time to go back inside, Alec stopped his go-cart. "Look, Grammy," he said, pointing to the sidewalk. "Daddy's heart." On the gray pavement lay a tiny red heart.

Several months after Bill's death it seemed to me that he was gone. I knew he was no longer around in his body, but I'd had a strong sense of his presence. But now I wasn't feeling that. I wondered about this. Should I let him go completely? I felt a sharp pain in my heart at the thought that he would disappear forever, that I'd never sense his presence ever again. And then I remembered that what I always wanted for my loved ones was whatever was best for them. If Bill was to go on, then I would let him do that. I felt a heavy sadness at the loss of his presence.

And then about ten days later, I dreamed of Bill again. Another lucid dream. He came to me, but he was different. He was about ten feet tall, wearing a long dark cape so that when he raised his arms, they looked like giant wings. I walked up to him, then turned so my back was against his body. He wrapped his arms about me so that only my head showed. I felt a wave of warmth and lightness go through my body. *He's back*, I thought. I've been strongly aware of his presence ever since.

Bill had let me know that I was "up for it"—for being the mother of a man who had committed suicide. I keep asking if I am. Am I willing to tell the truth about him and his death and still hold my head high and live? I'd better, if only for the memory of that son—my beautiful Bill. I will live with the dichotomy of having a son who was wonderful—all a mother could ever ask for—who at the same time has done a terrible thing, murdered himself. My grief is eased as I reach out to others in friendship and love. My family is close and loving. I draw on the strength and energy of a source greater than myself, on the ultimate power of the universe, on the mysteries that surround us. I live my life doing the best I can, forgiving myself when I fall short, and being "up for it."

Albert Einstein wrote to the children of his friend Besso, who died just 34 days before his own death, ". . . now he's gone slightly ahead of me again, leaving this strange world. That doesn't mean anything. For us believing physicists this separation between past and present and future has the value of mere illusion, however tenacious."

My son, now dead, has merely changed form. My experience of him lives on. As I had learned to communicate by phone, letter, email, and Skype, I would learn to stay in touch with my son who had "gone slightly ahead of me." I made no conscious plan to do so. I merely keep myself open to all possibilities, trusting that I might, as Rilke's poem says, "gradually, without noticing it, live along some distant day into the answer."[41]

If you've lost a loved one to suicide, my heart goes out to you. Your loved one is gone, the journey here for them complete. But you are still here, still on the journey of life, and your mandate is to live fully. I join with you in the request of the ages, "Requiem aeternam dona eis, et lux perpetua luceat eis." May they rest in peace forever, and let light perpetual shine upon them. And I am sure that as they passed over, all the trumpets in the heavenly realms sounded for them on the other side. We can join with Horatio as he says, "Good night, sweet prince, and flights of angels sing thee to thy rest!"[42]

Be willing to live with the unanswered questions and with your grief. Life is in constant movement, and one must be willing to go down avenues, walking through the open doors. Don't lock yourself away, no matter how comfortable that might be, for you close out the light of life.

I will live with the questions, not to be martyred or sad, but to be open—"to live the questions now." Tragedy is merely one of the components of life. We do not seek after pain and grief, but we do not live to avoid them either. Life is like a complicated dance, and the goal is not to avoid getting bumped or to analyze the tempo. Our task is to dance, getting back in step when we falter, picking up a new tempo when the tune is changed. While in this process called living I can never fully understand life. I merely can live. My challenge to you is to be patient and gentle with yourselves, and to live with the questions.

---

[41]   Rilke, p. 34

[42]   Shakespeare, *Hamlet*, Act V, Scene ii

References

Alcoholics Anonymous (1976) New York: Alcoholics Anonymous World Services, Inc.

Alvarez, A. (1971/1990) *The Savage God: A Study of Suicide*. New York: W.W. Norton & Company.

Bateson, Gregory. (1972) *Steps to an Ecology of Mind*. New York: Ballantine Books.

Buechner, Frederick. (1990) *Faces on Faith* Videorecording of interviews at The Parish of Trinity Church. New York: United Methodist Communications.

Capra, Fritjof. (1976) *The Tao of Physics*. New York: Bantam Books.

Capra, Fritjof. (1982) *The Turning Point*. New York: Bantam Books.

Church of England. (1992) *The Book of Common Prayer and Administration of the Sacraments and Other Rites and Ceremonies of the Church According to the Use of the Church of England*. Great Britain: Ebury Press.

Declaration of Independence

Donne, John. (1930) *Biathanatos: Reproduced from the First Edition With a Bibliographical Note by J. William Hebel*. New York: Facsimile Text Society.

Franklin, Jon. (1987) *Molecules of the Mind: The Brave New Science of Molecular Psychology*. New York: Atheneum.

Gawain, Shakti. (1978) *Creative Visualization*. Berkeley, CA: Whatever Pub.

Golas, Thaddeus. (1972) *The Lazy Man's Guide to Enlightenment*. Palo Alto, CA: Seed Center.

Haidt, Jonathan. (2005) *The Happiness Hypothesis: Finding Modern Truth in Ancient Wisdom*. New York: Basic Books.

Holy Bible (1953) Revised Standard Version. New York: Thomas Nelson & Sons

Jamison, Kay Redfield. (1999) *Night Falls Fast: Understanding Suicide*. New York: Random House.

Kipling, Rudyard. (1901) *Kim*. New York: Doubleday, Page & Co.

Koerner, Brendan. The last word: Why AA works (sometimes). *The Week*, July 23, 2010.

Marcus, Gary. (2004) *The Birth of the Mind*. New York: Basic Books.

Merriam-Webster's Collegiate Dictionary (Eleventh Edition) Springfield, Massachusetts: Merriam-Webster, Incorporated.

Munsch, Robert. (1986) *Love You Forever.*. Scarborough, Ontario, Canada: Firefly Books, Ltd.

Pagels, Heinz R. (1982) *The Cosmic Code: Quantum Physics as the Language of Nature*. New York: Simon and Schuster.

Paul Winter Consort. (1982) *Missa Gaia* (Earth Mass). New York: Living Music Records, Inc.

Pert, Candace B. (1997) *Molecules of Emotion: The Science Behind Mind-Body Medicine*. New York: Touchstone / Simon & Schuster Inc.

Plath, Sylvia. (2004) *Ariel: The Restored Edition*. New York: Harper Collins.

Restak, Richard M. (1984) *The Brain*. New York: Bantam Books.

Rilke, Rainer Maria, and Stephen Mitchell. (1986) *Letters to a Young Poet*. New York: Vintage.

Slater, Philip Elliot. (1977) *The Wayward Gate: Science and the Supernatural*. Boston: Beacon Press.

Speziali, Pierre, ed. (1972) *Albert Einstein, Michele Besso Correspondence 1903-1955*. Paris: Hermann.

Storr, Anthony. (1988) *Solitude: A Return to the Self*. New York: Ballantine Books.

Styron, William. (1990) *Darkness Visible: A Memoir of Madness*. New York: Random House.

The Seattle Times, April 23, 2006.

Winograd, Terry, and Fernando Flores. (1986) *Understanding Computers and Cognition: A New Foundation for Design*. Norwood, NJ: Ablex Pub. Corp.

Wright, Robert. (1994) *The Moral Animal: Evolutionary Psychology and Everyday Life*. New York: Vintage Books.

Zukav, Gary. (1979) *The Dancing Wu Li Masters: An Overview of the New Physics*. New York: William Morrow.

Zukav, Gary. (1989) *The Seat of the Soul*. New York: Simon & Schuster.

Websites:

http://www.ypps.org

http://www.kagyuoffice.org/kagyulineage

CPSIA information can be obtained at www.ICGtesting.com
Printed in the USA
LVOW06s1734061015

457152LV00003B/611/P